before baby

A step-by-step guide to making and freezing meals before your newborn makes cooking impossible

Autumn Hoverter, MS, RDN
with Ben Hoverter

food wise
nutrition

To Teo:
Who changed everything.

First edition published by FoodWise Nutrition, LLC, 2015.

The information in this book is not intended to be diagnostic or prescriptive.

Cover design by Ben Hoverter

ISBN-13: 978-1517343422

ISBN-10: 1517343429

BISAC: Cooking / General

FoodWise Nutrition, LLC

www.foodwisenutrtition.com

www.autumnhoverter.com

before baby
table of contents

an introduction

There are some very common experiences in adult life that we don't really talk about much.

One of those experiences hits right after your baby arrives, and you realize that you can't get a single thing done, not even something basic like feeding yourself. Most new parents have this experience – we got hints about it from our friends – but there seems to be a sense that "that's just how it has to be."

We're here to tell you that that isn't how it has to be. Not at all. You can eat well with a newborn. You just have to know what to do before your baby arrives!

We've developed and tested a method, a plan, and a set of surefire recipes that will fill your freezer with nourishing, dependable meals for when your baby arrives and you no longer have the time or energy to cook. We used this approach before our son was born, and we can't imagine doing it any other way. Our friends have tried it, and they won't ever go back to cold takeout and cereal dinners. You can do it too.

There's nothing esoteric about the method. Our whole approach is informed by Autumn's professional expertise in nutrition, but we arrived at a lot of the tricks and techniques here through trial and error. All of the recipes here are "rough-and-tumble," and can be modified according to your family's particular dietary needs and tastes. We do it all the time, and it works out just fine.

There's one area of expertise, though, where you should be careful, and that's food allergies and sensitivities. Even if you have no difficulty with food intolerance (gluten sensitivity, celiac disease, lactose intolerance, etc.), many newborns suffer from immune reactions to particular proteins passed through the mother's milk. When your baby suffers, so do you.

You won't know if your child has this problem until he or she is born, so we've designed each of these recipes to be naturally free of of major allergens for your baby's health and your peace of mind. There are no gluten-containing grains or dairy sources in Before Baby. We've also made each recipe with a vegan variant for those who prefer to avoid animal products. We believe that you shouldn't have to compromise your health or your food just because you're bringing a new human being into the world.

Ultimately, we want to give you the information and the power to shape your family's experience after your baby comes. It's a magical time. Be ready to enjoy it!

We waited a while to have kids.

So when Autumn finally got pregnant, we were exuberant. When she went into labor, we were excited. After pushing for four-and-a-half hours, we were exhausted. And when our son Teo was born, we were exhilarated.

But when he was diagnosed with intermittent left-side seizures, things fell apart.

Our first days after his birth were spent in the NICU with him, or in a family lounge, or grabbing fistfuls of sleep in spartan hospital lodgings. It was a strange time, and we relied almost completely on the kindness of friends and family to bring food, clothing, and the supplies we'd had no idea we would need when we packed for the hospital. They were our lifeline, our connection to the outside world. And boy, did they step up.

When we brought our son home, though, we'd relied so much on the kindness of friends and family that we felt we couldn't ask for more than the days and days of lunch and dinner they had already provided on short notice. We wanted to get on with the very adult business of feeding ourselves, but with a sick newborn, shopping and cooking took on a whole new dimension of challenge.

Fortunately, we were prepared.

During the last trimester of her pregnancy, Autumn had embarked on a voyage of culinary experimentation, using her kitchen expertise and her Master's degree in nutrition to develop recipes that would reheat well, taste delicious, and support our family's health with complete nutrients from whole foods.

She had filled our freezer. It was a thing of beauty.

Her preparation paid for itself many times over in the weeks after we brought our son home, and we want to share our methods with you. Even if your child comes into this world with all the grace of a star quarterback or prima ballerina, you'll want to eat well afterward, and that's a tall order with a newborn.

We can help you.

Yours in parenthood,

Autumn and Ben Hoverter

why prep?

"My baby never lets me cook!"

"I literally haven't eaten all day."

*"I love to cook, and I was always the one who prepared the meals. But if I don't do it, it doesn't get done…
and I just can't!"*

If you're reading this book, you may already know that cooking with a newborn is much harder than it looks. That alone is a great reason to prep food ahead of time, but here are some others you may not have considered:

1. Family members can only cook if they're around

If you have family members in the area and they're willing to become your personal chefs for a month, that's fantastic – glom on and don't let go! If, however, you have less family nearby (or they just aren't up to the task), then you have to be ready.

2. Friends only bring about a week's worth of food

We have marvelous friends. They're our family in the big bad city, and we depend on each other. We've cooked for them, and they've cooked for us, but the simple truth is that everyone has a life, so it isn't reasonable to expect a month of meals from your friends.

It seems like the average contribution from a friend group is a week, maybe two. That's wonderful help – take it! But get prepared for the month after the friend-food runs out.

3. Prepping is much cheaper than buying meals

Go price a month of lunches and dinners for your family out of the grocery freezer case. Go ahead – I'll wait. Then, when you've recovered from sticker shock, recognize: *that's the alternative to cooking*. Prep your own meals and your bank account will thank you.

4. Food you cook is just plain better, and better for your family, too

We love to eat out, and we eat frozen meals from time to time, too. There are nights when it's great not to have to think about dinner! But whether it's a frozen meal or a four-star feast, a meal you buy is a meal built to keep you coming back for more. That means too much of everything – salt, fat, sugar – and not enough of the humble ingredients that make a meal truly nourishing. How many vegetables went into that can of chili? Do you even know what sodium benzoate *does?*

5. Exhaustion breeds bad choices

Would you go shop for a car after getting only 3 hours of sleep a night for a week? I hope not!
We all recognize that it gets harder and harder to think clearly as you become exhausted, and meal planning takes work at the best of times. You want the planning work out of the way, along with the cooking!

6. Dietary restrictions make helping out hard

If you're vegetarian, vegan, gluten-intolerant, dairy-intolerant, or observe other specific dietary constraints, you already know that friends and family don't always "get it." That makes accepting their help tricky, and it puts them in a difficult position when they want to feed you. Taking control of your own cooking before the baby arrives eliminates all the questions. It's just simpler!

What Moms Say:

"After I had my daughter Flora, I thought a slow cooker would be a great idea, so I asked my husband to go pick one up. He did – he picked out a really nice one – and then it sat unopened for two weeks. I couldn't find the time or energy to open it!"

- Katie S.

- 1 -

basic nutrition

I'm a practicing dietitian, so I know how challenging it can be to separate fact from fiction when it comes to healthy eating. Put your mind at ease, though, because all the recipes in this book have my stamp of approval, and they're delicious too.

However, I want to empower you to make decisions about **all** your food rather than depending on the recipes I've provided. After all, there's breakfast to consider, and snacks! Your baby's long-term health – and your own – relies on you making good decisions, starting now.

Here are two big considerations for the weeks after your baby is born:

Consideration #1: The Healthy Plate

Remember the old FDA food pyramid? We don't use that anymore. Instead, we use a much simpler, more flexible model called the Healthy Plate.

The standard version has half your plate covered in veggies, plus a fruit and a glass of milk thrown in, but we're going to change that. For postpartum ease, we're going to use a simplified plate filled with one-third each of veggies, protein, and carbohydrates. To make it even easier, most of my recipes are one-pot meals that will satisfy both your nutrition needs and your taste buds while fulfilling the Healthy Plate requirements. Most of the recipes provide more vegetables than this model, but we want to take the pressure off during your first month with a newborn!

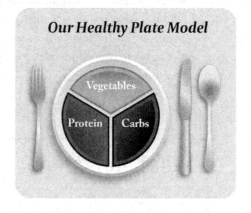

Our Healthy Plate Model

Consideration #2: Feeling Full

The sense of fullness that says you've actually gotten enough to eat is called *satiety*, and it's crucial. Without it, you'll tend to keep snacking or eating sweets to satisfy your hunger, and that often ends with a tub of Ben & Jerry's, which is... not ideal.

To make sure your meal fills you up and keeps you from getting hungry an hour later, it needs to contain four components: fiber, fat, protein, and complex carbohydrates.

"But wait," you say, "my Atkins/Paleo/South Beach diet says I don't need carbs, and that diet keeps me full/helps me lose weight!"

I get that. Under other circumstances, I would tell you that low- or no-carb diets can be temporarily safe, and they can lead to temporary fat loss. However, you're going to have a baby! Your priority after delivery has to be your family's health and energy level, and a low-carb diet won't support those as well as a diet rich in complex carbohydrates (which is really just another way of saying, "eat whole grains.")

Carbs are an excellent source of the calories mom will need while breastfeeding, and whole grains contain B-vitamins and minerals that support your energy, immune system, and mood. They'll help keep you full, and the fiber present in most complex carbs will help prevent constipation – which is priceless when you've just given birth!

Nutrition Q & A

What's a good carb?

Carbs get an unnecessarily bad rap. Ultimately, all starches get broken down into glucose, which is your body's preferred fuel source – it's crucial for the proper function of your brain and nervous system, as well as red and white blood cell production. An average adult requires a minimum of about 130 grams of glucose per day from food; for lactating women, this jumps to about 210 grams per day.

That said, some carbs turn into glucose more slowly, which helps keep your blood sugar and mood more even. These whole-food carb sources also contain fiber and micronutrients that will do you a world of good. If you're looking for high-quality carbs, look for brown whole grains and whole grain flours, as well as starchy vegetables like squash and potatoes. There are also quality carbs to be found in beans and lentils. Just remember: the whiter the flour, the more processed it is, and the less nutrition it contains.

When your child arrives, keep in mind that you'll need more calories and nutrients, too, and complex carbohydrates are a great way to get both. Expect to need about 500 more calories per day while breastfeeding, and re-member: a mother's diet directly impacts the nutritional value of her milk!

Why bother with fiber?

If you eat plants, you get fiber. Period. Hence all the veggies in these recipes! That said, there are two different kinds of fiber, and they serve different but equally import-ant purposes in the body.

First is *soluble fiber*. This kind of fiber soaks up water and prevents diarrhea, but there's another reason why it's great: it binds cholesterol and carries it away!

Second is *insoluble fiber*, which is useful because it gives digested food bulk, and that prevents constipation by giving your digestive tract something to push.

However, insoluble fiber has a second and more critical function: it also feeds the beneficial bacteria in your colon, and there's more and more evidence that healthy gut bacteria have a huge positive effect on human health. If mom experienced a difficult delivery or received antibiotics, fiber will help with the recovery of her digestive tract, and maybe her whole body!

Last, fiber keeps you feeling full longer, which prevents that unfortunate Ben & Jerry's binge at 11:00 p.m. and staves off the irritability that goes along with hunger. When your nerves are already frayed from sleepless nights and a fussy newborn, that's priceless.

So what's a good protein?

Meat (including fish) is the easiest source of complete protein for humans, and it comes with some vitamins that are difficult to get from any other food (like B-12, iron, and zinc).

However, there are many other great sources of protein besides meat: eggs, soy, beans and lentils, seeds and nuts, and dairy all contain significant quantities of protein that your body can use to build itself. You have lots of options!

What about vegetarian protein sources?

When you're vegetarian or vegan, the name of the game is getting enough complete protein from your diet, and that means eating foods containing all the amino acids your body can't manufacture on its own. Because very few plant sources of protein contain all these "essential" amino acids, you have to assemble a complete set from several foods.

It can also be challenging to eat enough protein during the day because vegetarian protein sources are more difficult for your body to use than animal proteins. Fortunately, you don't have to eat all your proteins in one meal – there's nothing wrong with eating different protein sources throughout your day. In fact, eating a variety of protein foods is the best and simplest way to make sure you're getting everything you need to build your body and keep it strong.

If you've been vegetarian or vegan for a long time, you probably feel like you have a good sense of how much protein your body needs. However, it's worth reviewing the list below, especially if you're breastfeeding!

Remember, every...	...has this much protein:
4 ounces of firm tofu	13 grams
½ cup of cooked whole beans	7 grams
½ cup of cooked lentils	9 grams
1 cup of milk	8 grams
1 cup of soy milk	7 grams
1 whole egg	7 grams
¼ cup of nuts	8 grams
2 tablespoons of seeds	3 grams
2 tablespoons of nut butter	8 grams
½ cup of cooked quinoa	4 grams
½ cup of cooked rice	3 grams

QUICK TIP

1 ounce of meat, fish or poultry has about 7 grams of protein.

To figure out how much protein you need, use this simple calculation:

Your pre-pregnancy weight in pounds ÷ 2.2
= Grams of protein you need per day

If you're used to kilograms, you don't need to do any math at all – your pre-pregnancy weight in kilos is the same as the grams of protein you need in a day!

What's a healthy fat?

Fat is extremely important. After all, your brain is made largely out of fat! However, there's quite a bit of debate about what the best fats are. At this point, we know a few things:

First off, don't burn your fats when cooking. Heating oil to the smoke point changes its molecular structure and makes it much, much more likely to cause inflammation and sticky arteries, which in turn lead to atherosclerosis and other diseases. Use refined safflower, sunflower, avocado or coconut oils for high-heat cooking instead. They'll hold up better.

The general rule for choosing fats is this: ***plant over animal***. Most plant-based fats are unsaturated and anti-inflammatory, while most animal fats are saturated and pro-inflammatory. Fish oils buck this trend; they're one of the few animal fats that seems to soothe inflammation in the body, rather than aggravating it, and that's great for your heart health and general well-being, so long as you use them in moderation.

Please understand that the saturated fats common in animal foods (meats, dairy, eggs) are useful for your body in moderate amounts. You need cholesterol. You need saturated fat. But eating more than you need won't pay off in the long run!

So what do you do? Well, fats from fish, flax, chia and walnuts are high in the crucial omega-3 fatty acids, and they're very anti-inflammatory, so use them freely. When you need a high-heat oil, you can choose from refined safflower or sunflower oils. For medium heat, coconut oil is a good choice; although it contains saturated fat, its benefits far outweigh its costs. Avoid lard, and only use olive oil for low-heat cooking so it doesn't burn. Eat a little less meat and a few more plants. Nuts are great.

That's about it.

Here are the fats to keep in your cupboard:

- **Extra virgin olive oil** for low-heat cooking
- **Extra virgin coconut oil** for medium-heat cooking
- **Refined safflower** or **sunflower oil** for high-heat cooking
- **Flax oil** for delicious dressings or as a garnish, *never for cooking!*

What's a good vegetable?

A good vegetable is any vegetable you will eat. Seriously! Your goal is to eat veggies in a wide range of colors to get the most nutrients, but don't force yourself to eat something you don't like. You may also discover that it's cheaper or easier to eat seasonally: apples and squash might feature prominently in your diet during the fall and winter, while greens and berries may become a staple during the late spring and summer. Fruits and vegetables are less expensive when they're in season, and they taste better too!

What are "micronutrients"?

Every process in the body requires vitamins, minerals, and other bioactive compounds, and these are all classed together as micronutrients. Most of these compounds come from the fruits and vegetables we eat. Many come specifically from the different *colors* that we eat, because the color compounds in fruits and vegetables are nutrients too!

Vitamins are chemicals our cells can't manufacture, and minerals are the less-common elements used in our biochemistry. We have to get both from our foods. Fruits and veggies provide most of the vitamins and minerals in our diets, although grains are our major source of B-vitamins (the "energy" vitamins). Nuts and seeds are also excellent sources of some minerals, and they're chock-full of healthy fats. And meats, especially lean meats, are a great source of iron and zinc, which are crucial for mom and baby. Red meat is also high in vitamin B-12, which is nearly impossible to get from plant sources (vegetarians and vegans, take note).

It should come as no surprise, then, that the best way to get all these micronutrients in your diet is to eat a variety of foods, including lots of fruits and vegetables, complex whole-grain carbohydrates, nuts and seeds, and lean meats. And on that count, these recipes have you covered!

How do food allergies work in infants?

One of the ways your food affects your baby is through food intolerances and allergies. Many children have no such problems, but some mothers find that if they eat certain foods or drink certain beverages, it causes their baby distress. There's no way to guess whether this will be the case for your family, so I've built my recipes to be free of common problem foods.

There's a big difference between an allergy and an intolerance. An allergy is an obvious immune response like a runny nose, scratchy throat, shortness of breath, or, in the most severe cases, an anaphylactic reaction (which requires immediate medical attention). Food allergies typically develop when the child starts eating food on her own, so this is unlikely to be a problem for your first few months.

Food intolerance, though, can be an issue from the start. When mom eats food, some of the proteins and other compounds from that food get passed along in her milk, and those compounds can cause an immune reaction in your child. It's a non-anaphylactic reaction that isn't life-threatening, but it can cause significant discomfort for your baby, which translates into discomfort for you.

Common symptoms of food intolerance may include:

- **Eczema**
- **Reflux/Regurgitation**
- **Frequent gas**
- **Unexplained fussiness**
- **Trouble sleeping**
- **Diarrhea or constipation**

The most common culprits in infant food intolerance seem to be gluten and dairy, though soy and caffeine can contribute as well. All our recipes are naturally gluten-, dairy- and soy-free (unless you substitute soy), so you'll be well on your way to preventing food issues with your infant by using them. Make sure to keep a careful eye on your child when you start eating more inclusive fare, though.

How do the recipes accomplish all this?

First, I've doubled or tripled the amount of veggies in each of these recipes. Eat the meal and you'll get all the vitamins and minerals you need.

Second, most of these are one-pot meals. Each dish is automatically a healthy plate.

Third, for the meals that aren't one-pot, you'll be blanching or microwaving frozen vegetables to add. Don't skip them – you'll thank me later!

So, what's the bottom line?

The bottom line is **"whole foods."** Not the grocery chain, the *concept!* Basically, if you don't recognize it as the product of a once-living thing, don't eat it. Food is vegetables. It is beans. It is nuts and seeds. It is whole grains, and flours made from them. It is eggs. It is meat. It is milk and cheese, if you can tolerate them. It is fruit. These are the things to feed your family, both for your own health and the

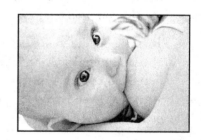

health of your new baby, who relies on you for 100% of his or her nutrition.

New mothers need about 500 extra calories per day while breastfeeding, and that translates into a lot of extra food. Mom can get it easily if she's eating junk food, but remember: mom's diet will directly impact the nutritional quality of her milk. Junk food has calories, but very few nutrients. **So put good food in the freezer!**

– 2 –

how to freeze

Freezing food is the simplest thing in the world, but not many people do it. I think most people are intimidated – worried that the food will spoil, concerned about allergens, afraid the food won't taste good when they reheat it. But fear no more! Most foods freeze and reheat well. You don't need special packaging or preservatives to make delicious and nutritious frozen meals for you and your family. However, a few foods will break down in the freezer, and others require care to ensure your safety when you reheat them, so a little know-how will help a lot.

It's a double-edged sword

Freezing stops the chemical processes in food that would lead to spoilage, but it does this at a cost: ice crystals form during freezing, and they damage the microscopic structure of your food. This means that frozen foods will often leak fluid when they thaw, or lose the good texture of their fresh counterparts. Neither result will be an issue for these recipes, but if you intend to freeze your own, keep this effect in mind!

What is freezer burn?

Freezer burn, the whitish discoloration on frozen foods, occurs because of exposure to air at low temperatures. Many people find that it lends foods an "off" flavor that is undesirable, if tolerable. Some air exposure is inevitable during the freezing process, but it can be minimized with a little forethought. We'll be removing as much air as possible from our dishes to prevent freezer burn – don't skip that step!

So, what can I freeze?

You can freeze anything that isn't in a can (or a shell – eggs don't freeze well). Meats, grains, spices, and even fruits and most vegetables, will all freeze well. However, some foods lose their textures or flavors during an extended stay in the freezer, so I've avoided those in these recipes.

What Freezes?	What Doesn't?
Fruits and veggies *(to be cooked later)*	Fruits and veggies *(to be eaten raw)*
Bread products	Whole potatoes
Meats *(cooked or raw)*	Previously frozen fish
Cooked grains	Pre-cooked pasta
Cooked beans	Dairy products
Soups and stews	Mayonnaise
Berries	Jellies

The Right Way to Freeze

I'm going to outline a six-step process that gives you great results every time. The first step is the most crucial.

Step One: Start cooling it

Once you've prepared your food, you need to cool it down quickly. After I've prepared a dish, I transfer it into large metal bowls and stir it frequently to help it cool. For every large batch of soup or stew I prepare, I generally cool it in 2 or 3 smaller containers. Metal bowls are ideal because they transfer heat well, but you can also use plastic bowls or large pots. The goal is to get your food out of the pot and into a thin-walled container that will allow the heat to dissipate.

In large industrial kitchens or restaurants they cool food in large, flat metal containers no more than 3 inches deep. This is probably ideal, but I have nowhere to store such containers, and I certainly don't have the fridge space! If you are inclined in this direction, restaurant supply chains like Cash and Carry sell these large containers dirt cheap.

Remember: Don't leave your food on the counter for more than 2 hours or you run the risk of bacterial contamination! In the next chapter I discuss food safety, and that's the key to preventing unwanted microbial growth and keeping your family healthy.

Step Two: *Label your containers*

While your food starts cooling, label your bags or containers with a Sharpie. Write down the name of the food, the date you made it, and the quantity (it's easy to measure as you're filling each container). You need to know!

Also, write down how you're supposed to reheat each meal – you don't want to have to remember. For the recipes in this book, you'll usually just thaw the food in the fridge and then heat it on the stovetop or microwave.

Step Three: *Fill it up*

Once your food has cooled (remember, it won't be cold, or even room temperature), put it in the container you plan to freeze it in. You have lots of options for freezing containers, including plastic containers, glass jars, and freezer bags. I prefer freezer bags because they stack easily and thaw easily too, but the other containers work just fine. If you are using a glass or metal container, remember to leave ½- to 1-inch of air at the top of the container. Your food will expand when frozen!

If you're using plastic or glass containers, a canning funnel may be helpful. If you're using plastic bags (which I prefer), fold down the top third of the bag to keep it cleaner, then hold the bag open and upright on the counter with one hand, and dump with the other hand!. If you're using smaller bags, I suggest placing the empty bag in a tall plastic cup and folding the edges over the cup's lip before filling it. Works great.

Only fill your bags up to the halfway point! You want them to lay flat in the freezer for easy stacking. Be consistent, so you know how much to defrost.

Step Four: Cool it in the fridge

Seal the bag and flatten it out on a cookie sheet, then find it a home in the refrigerator. Let it cool completely in the fridge, 4-6 hours for a 2-quart bag of food. Never put hot food directly into the freezer! If you do, you'll raise the temperature of the whole freezer and potentially spoil the other foods that you've already frozen.

Once you've filled a bag, there's a trick to minimizing both the space it takes up and its chances of freezer burn: suck out the air! Seal it almost completely except for a small opening in the middle, then push gently inward from both sides of the opening to spread it apart. Lock your lips around it and suck out as much air as you can! No, I'm not kidding. It works like a charm, and it will minimize the space each bag takes up, as well as reducing the likelihood of ice crystals and freezer burn inside your bags. If you're not thrilled with the idea of putting your mouth on a bag of food, you can use a straw to suck out the air instead – it takes a little more care, but eliminates any transfer of saliva.

Step Five: Freeze it flat

You may need to suck out the air again if there's a lot left. Then lay the cookie sheet in your freezer for 8 hours. If necessary, you can usually stack flattened bags three deep on a cookie sheet for freezing, as long as you're careful not to let them slide off.

Step Six: Stack it!

Stack your flat, frozen food in the freezer. Our freezer's shelves were just a bit too short to stack the bags vertically, but I would recommend it if you can, as much for ease of access as for the joy of stacking meals like books on a shelf!

Keep in mind that different meals should be frozen in the quantities you will use at a time. Two quarts of soup can be thawed and eaten in one or two meals by most families, but if you put two quarts of pasta sauce in a bag, that's quite a bit of sauce to thaw and use before it spoils! Usually, don't put more than 2 quarts in a gallon freezer bag, as it won't freeze or thaw as easily. If you have a big family (or big eaters!), you're better off thawing more than one bag at a time rather than trying to put more food in each bag. Always ask yourself: **"Will I use all of it after I thaw it?"**

So... What's "Proper" Freezing?

If you want to keep the colors, flavors, textures, and nutrient value of your frozen foods intact, you have to freeze them at 0° F or colder. What's more, you want to freeze raw foods at their peak freshness; foods near the end of their shelf life aren't as resilient to freezing and thawing. If you're freezing cooked meals (as we do in many of the stove-top recipes), freeze ASAP after the food has cooled. Waiting won't make it better!

Ideally, you want your food to freeze quickly, too. The longer an item takes to freeze, the more "jagged" ice crystals form, and they tend to destroy the structure of the food, which makes it mealy or dry when reheated. When you lay out a half-full gallon bag of soup the way I've described, it freezes in about an hour, nice and quick. Follow the directions and you'll be fine!

A Few Key Tricks

1. **Squeeze or suck most of the air out of bags of soup or stew**, just as I've described. This minimizes the space for ice crystals to form.

2. **Leave an inch or so at the top of mason jars.** You want to give the contents room to expand as they freeze – broken jars mean wasted food.

3. **Steer clear of casseroles.** It isn't random chance that none of the recipes in this book are casseroles: they inevitably have air left between the lid and the surface of the food, and that tends to lead to freezer burn, which we'd like to avoid. If you want to make casseroles to freeze (or if family brings them as a favor), here's the trick: let the casserole freeze, then tightly cover the surface with plastic wrap, pressing it down on top to minimize air contact. Then crumple up wax paper on top of the plastic between the casserole and the lid. This is a low-effort way to keep freezer burn at bay!

What if your family doesn't like leftovers?

Each of these recipes is designed to make between 2 and 4 quarts of food. Your family will determine how many meals that translates to, but a good rule is that a single serving is about 2 cups of soup or stew, or 1 cup of pasta sauce. I recommend serving one of the recipes without freezing, just to see how much you'll need per serving.

If leftovers don't fly at your house, just freeze each batch of food in 1-quart bags (half full!) rather than gallon-size freezer bags. That way, each bag contains one serving of soup or stew, or two servings of pasta sauce. Voila! A different dinner each night. And the same principle holds for lunches: if you don't want leftovers for lunch, just take out two different meals to thaw at a stretch – one for dinner, one for tomorrow's lunch!

Maximizing a Small Space

Avoid mason jars if you have a small freezer–use bags instead. All that glass takes up space!

Also, if you have a small freezer, beware casseroles. They're very popular items for friends and family to bring over, but casseroles are bulky, and they can't be tailored to the serving sizes you desire or the dimensions of your freezer the way a bag of soup or stew can. I suggest eating them as soon as you can so they don't consume valuable freezer space.

And since we're talking about freezing, we also need to talk about…

– 3 –

food safety

Food safety should be a priority, whether you're cooking for 5 or 500. Even minor food-borne illness can put your family out of commission, and that's time you could be spending with your baby!

The Two Rules for Freezing Safely

Rule One: Your freezer gets cold and stays cold.

Your freezer is doing its job if it keeps food at or below 0 degrees Fahrenheit, or -18 degrees Celsius. This temperature ensures that your foods never come close to thawing, which is crucial because you can't let frozen food thaw without allowing some bacterial growth. After all, freezing keeps foods fresh by stopping the activity of microorganisms that would otherwise cause food to spoil and make you sick. If your stored food begins to thaw, it's time to go the rest of the way: cook and eat it! Refreezing thawed food, especially raw food, leads to illness.

Rule Two: The food was safe to begin with!

If you made that delicious soup, then accidentally left it on the stove to cool for, oh, 10 hours, then I'm sorry, that soup is not safe – whether or not it gets frozen! Remember that freezing doesn't kill most microorganisms, it just puts them in "suspended animation," ready to wreak havoc when they get warm again. Cool your cooked foods quickly, then put them in the fridge. Freeze ASAP.

Generally, the foods in this book will keep for 2-3 months in the freezer. If you receive or make casseroles, eat them before your soups and stews. The extra air exposure will tend to freezer-burn casseroles quickly.

How to Thaw

There are three main ways to thaw your food safely, but first, I must admit that I have sometimes ignored my own advice and left frozen chicken to thaw on a countertop. Don't do it! If you do, you're playing Russian Roulette with salmonella (or worse). Be smarter than me and use one of these three safe methods to thaw your food:

Method One: Put it in a plastic bag and submerge it in cold water.

 This method is my favorite because it's easy and fairly quick. You'll have to change the water every half-hour or so to keep it thawing, and please make sure water isn't getting in, or the results will be unpleasant. Once the food is thawed enough to break apart, you can often transfer it straight to a pot, bowl or plate and heat it the rest of the way!

Method Two: Put it in the fridge and wait.

 This takes a little planning, but most of these recipes can thaw enough to cook easily during a 12-hour overnight stay in the fridge. I always put a cookie sheet beneath food I thaw this way – it makes cleanup easier if the plastic bag has developed any holes during freezing.

Method Three: Microwave it.

 After thawing in the microwave, cook the food immediately. You don't want to bring the temperature up, then give microorganisms time to grow! But a warning: never microwave plastic. It breaks the plastic down, which puts more toxins into your food. If you're going to microwave, use glass or ceramic.

Food Safety Q & A

Can I put frozen food in the slow cooker?

Formal food safety advice says never to put any frozen food in the slow cooker. It takes a long time to heat up, which means that it stays at a bacteria-friendly temperature for way too long. What I've found is that I can get away using a little frozen food, like a bag of peas, as long as the rest of the ingredients come from the fridge or the cupboard. Never, ever put an entire frozen meal in the slow cooker.

Does freezing impact food quality?

Freezing properly has surprisingly little effect on the quality of most foods, but the key word here is "properly." How you thaw makes a difference, too, so be sure to follow the directions above!

Can I refreeze?

The short answer is, "Yes." The longer answer is, "Yes, but are you sure you want to?" Refreezing often leads to dry meats and mushy vegetables. However, it's safe as long as you refreeze cooked foods by the end of their fourth day in the fridge. But if you left them out of the fridge for more than two hours, then you shouldn't be freezing them – you've given bacteria too much time to grow.

If you thawed too many uncooked bags of food and want to refreeze some, you can, so long as they haven't gone above normal refrigerator temperatures (40° F / 4° C). Be forewarned, though: the quality of the food will probably suffer.

What if I have a power outage?

Don't panic. Breathe. You've prepared a lot of food, and it may not go to waste if you're careful. Rather than opening the freezer to reorganize it, leave it closed. It's well-insulated and it's full of cold water-based food that will warm slowly. It will be fine for one or two days *if* you don't start pulling things out. The more food in the freezer, the better; a full freezer takes up to twice as long to warm as a half-empty one.

Will storing food in plastic leach chemicals into my food?

The short answer is that yes, if your food is touching plastic, a small number of plastic molecules will migrate into your food. It's unavoidable. Everytime we purchase a package of quinoa or place bulk nuts in a plastic bag, a small amount of plastic leaches into the food. Period.

So, how much is migrating in? To date, there are no studies that can answer this question definitively, but what we do know is that you shouldn't heat food in plastic if you can possibly avoid it. The heat destabilizes the molecules in the plastic and increases their rate of transfer into your food.

Now, I know that the real question you have about plastic storage is: "*Will I do my baby irreparable harm?*" And the answer is… I don't know. Science doesn't have a clear answer. Less plastic is certainly better, but how much less? You'll have to make that call for yourself.

When you're deciding how to store your food in the freezer, keep in mind that this one decision probably isn't going to make or break your body's toxicity. Chemical buildup is cumulative, and based on all the toxic exposure you experience during the course of your day, your year, and your lifetime. It's the flame retardant sprayed into your new couch. It's the exhaust from the cars on your street. It's the industrial contamination in your water. In the grand scheme of things, *freezing* your food in plastic (and reheating it in pans or bowls) barely rates.

Your liver possesses a system, the cytochrome P450 system, that detoxifies all these chemicals and gets them out of your body, but it's possible to overwhelm the system. The best way to support this system is to eat a lot of fruits, veggies, whole grains, nuts and seeds, drink lots of water, and, of course, limit exposure. Only you can decide if freezing in plastic will "break the bank." If you are very concerned, freeze in glass jars; they don't have the associated toxicity concerns.

And speaking of the "plastic or glass?" question, let's talk about...

– 4 –

gearing up

To do this right, you'll need some gear. It falls into two main categories: storage containers and kitchen implements.

Storing Food: The Right Stuff

It's surprisingly simple to freeze and store food if you choose the meals carefully. Everything in this book is designed to fit in one of two types of containers until it gets reheated; those containers are **gallon plastic bags** (available at the grocery store) or **quart mason jars** (sometimes available at the grocery store, otherwise at big-box stores). Along with these containers, it will be helpful to have some plastic wrap (like Saran-wrap) and aluminum foil on hand.

Kitchen tools: What you need

There's a practical kitchen, and then there's a luxury kitchen. To prep using this book, you need the first one, not the second. Don't stress out if you don't think your kitchen is perfect, because it doesn't have to be. Mine sure isn't!

You'll only need three big items. They are:

- **A slow cooker,** 6 quart minimum. 4 quarts will be too small for our purposes.

- **A large, deep saucepan or stockpot**, 6-8 quarts. (You'll want two pots if you're doing more than one recipe at a time on the stovetop)

- **A sharp chef's knife.** I love my $40 Victorinox. If yours is dull, save yourself a big headache and get it sharpened before starting to cook.

Honestly, you can probably make do with what you've got, so long as it will handle the quantity of food you'll be making.

You'll also need:

- **A cutting board** (preferably a big one)
- **Stirring spoons**
- **Mixing bowls**
- **A ladle**
- **A sieve/strainer** (both fine mesh and large holes)
- **And a set of measuring cups** (for solid and liquid) and spoons.

    Optional but handy: Canning funnel, Food scale, Garlic press, Food processor.

And remember: old equipment – stuff you know you can depend on – is best.

How to Use the Freezer You Have

You're going to need the freezer space to accommodate what you cook!

The first real question is this: how much space do you have access to? Do you have a fridge-freezer combo? Do you have an upright freezer? A chest freezer? What can it hold?

This is a harder question to answer than you might think. Freezers are usually measured in cubic feet, but that doesn't translate well to "quantity of frozen soup." So here's how to figure out how many meals your freezer can store.

Step One: Get rid of all unnecessary food.

Use up anything that is older than six months, and toss anything that's over a year old. We had a package of cocoa nibs stuck in the back of the freezer – I have no idea why – so I used them in cookies before our baby arrived. Every bit of space counts!

Once you've cleaned out your freezer, take a look at how much space you have and decide how much store-bought frozen food you can't live without. Our recipes will feed you dinners for a month, but if you need sweet potato fries and ice cream, that's going to take up space too. You probably already have the frozen foods you like to eat, so find them a spot in the freezer and work around them. I recommend taking extra frozen foods out of bulky packaging to save space, but if you do, write down the preparation instructions or tape them to the plastic wrap before you throw out the package!

And remember, using freezer bags to store your food will get you the most bang for your buck. It'll let you stack packages of food in your freezer/fridge combo without having to fight for space.

Step Two: Estimate the number of recipes your freezer can hold

1. **Get out the gallon bags.**

   Fill four of them halfway with water, flatten, and freeze flat (see *Chapter 2: How to Freeze* for more info). Four half-gallons is eight quarts, which is about what each recipe makes.

2. **Take your frozen bags of water to the freezer and stack them.**

   If you have to take other stuff out to see how they fit, that's fine, the water isn't staying.

3. **Ask: "How many groups of four could I fit on this shelf?"**

   Estimate across the shelf, then see if you could fit another set behind those, or in front. Your estimate doesn't have to be perfect – if you're a couple bags over, you'll be able to manage.

4. **Write down how many *four-bag recipes* you made fit on one shelf.**

   To estimate the number of recipes your freezer will accomodate, simply multiply the number of four-bag recipes per shelf by your number of shelves. *That's how many recipes your freezer accommodates.*

The reason we use gallon bags is that they provide the densest method of storing food in the freezer. If you're using mason jars, you need to try stacking them on a freezer shelf in much the same way.

Should I get a second freezer?

Ask yourself: *"Will I use a second freezer after my baby arrives?"* It's an expense, to be sure, and it takes up room. Unless you want a freezer for the future, I would strongly recommend that you try to make do with what you already have. We have a second freezer in the basement, but that doesn't make sense for every family.

However, many people discover they want more food on hand after baby comes. We've always enjoyed preserving the summer's bounty of berries, but now we also tend to keep a larger stock of frozen veggies and premade meals on hand for when things go awry (yes, I've continued making and freezing food since my little guy was born). There will be days when the doctor's appointment will take three times longer than expected, and then your little darling will refuse to nap, making preparing dinner difficult. Having a bit of extra food on hand can save everyone's sanity.

And once your freezer is ready, it's time to think about...

– 5 –

prep timelines

How much time do you need to set aside to make all this food? There are probably as many ways to plan your cooking as there are people, but I've outlined three main ways to do it.

Regardless of how you schedule your cooking, you'll want to look at your energy level, availability, and current level of cooking ability. Take a moment to consider the following questions.

- **Are you free on the weekends? Evenings? Daytime during the week?**

- **What's your energy level like? Are you at your best in the morning or evening?**

- **Do you do a lot of cooking already? Are you confident that you can juggle multiple tasks, or do you need to concentrate on one dish at a time?**

Keep in mind that pregnancy brain is real, and you may be "spacey." I burned more dishes while pregnant than during the entire rest of my life.

Bearing the above factors in mind, I've given you options!

They are:

 5-Week Prep: For those of you with plenty of lead time who want to space your cooking out.

 2-Week Prep: For those with less lead time, but a good deal of time to spend per day.

 5-Day Intensive: For those with a baby coming very soon, or those who just want it done!

Here's how each one works:

5-Week Prep

In the 5 week prep, you'll be cooking one recipe a day for two days a week, or cooking two recipes on a single day each week.

How do you decide? This will depend mostly on your energy level and ability to balance multiple tasks at once. If you are cooking one day per week, I suggest you cook one meal in the slow cooker and another on the stove – start the slow cooker recipe first and then move onto the stove-top recipe. I recommend grocery shopping the night before so you can start first thing in the morning.

Either way, start by choosing the ten recipes you want to prepare. As an example, let's say I've chosen my ten recipes, and the first two are Split Pea with Ham and Traditional Beef Stew.

I've decided that Saturday is my cooking day, so I go shopping Friday night with list in hand. Saturday morning I pull out the slow cooker and start the Split Pea with Ham. I get that recipe cooking, then I move straight into the prep for my stovetop dish, Traditional Beef Stew, and start heating my pot. I cook my stovetop dish, then I pull it off the stove and start cooling it (see *Chapter 2: How to Freeze*). While it cools, I make sure I have my freezer bags ready and freezer space available.

Once my slow cooker dish is done, I start cooling it too. That afternoon/evening, I set aside 30 minutes to bag each dish and get it freezing, then do clean up.

Then I'm done for that week! I'll go shopping next Friday to do it again. In five weeks, I'll be ready!

2-Week Prep

Here, you'll be cooking one recipe per day for five days in a row, taking a weekend break, and cooking for another five days. Choose your recipe order and go for it!

The approach to cooking in the 2-Week Prep is very similar to the 5-Week Prep. You're cooking only one recipe a day, though, so you'll be done sooner each day. This works great if you want to do something outside of the kitchen!

The other big difference is the shopping. You won't need to shop every evening if you *buy three recipes ahead*. List them out, buy the food, and you'll only need three shopping trips (or four, if you forget things like I do).

5-Day Intensive

Here, you'll be cooking two recipes a day for five days in a row. The daily process is identical to the two-a-day approach in the 5-Week Prep. Expect to cook one slow cooker dish and one stovetop dish per day.

The shopping for this prep timeline is pretty intense. I tried to buy ingredients for all ten dishes in one trip, and it's just too many groceries – remember, even if you can fit them all in your car, you need somewhere to keep the ingredients before you use them!

Instead, I suggest that you buy the ingredients for your first six dishes in one trip; this will prepare you for your first three days of cooking. You'll then make one more trip to the store later on, between day three and day four, so you can buy the ingredients for the remaining four dishes. This should keep the quantity manageable. Break it up further if you have the need and the time to do so.

The 5-Day Intensive takes some work, and it costs some money up front, but you'll be done before you know it! I don't recommend it in the last month or two of your pregnancy if your energy is low, but if you're highly energetic you can still pull it off!

What To Cook With What

If you're cooking two recipes per day, you can choose any two that strike your fancy, but be aware that some recipes are easier to prepare together than others. I've paired the recipes below to show you which ones share prep, ingredients, or other character- istics that make your workflow easier. Almost all of these recipes work in either the slow cooker or on the stovetop, but if I were to divide them up so I was cooking two per day, this is how I'd do it:

Cook two dishes at the same time!

In the Slow Cooker		*On the Stovetop*
Asian Pork		Sweet & Sour Chicken
Curry Vegetable Soup		White Bean Cassoulet
Chipotle Chili		Coconut Chicken Soup
Split Pea with Ham	*with*	Traditional Beef Stew
Beef with Kasha Soup		Red Lentil Soup
Country Chicken Stew		Adobo Corn Chowder
Black Bean Soup		Beef Ragu

*...and cook the **Chicken Peanut Stew** either way!*

— 6 —

using your meals

So, you did all the prep, you had your baby, and now you're ready to eat! How do you space your meals to get the most out of your preparation?

The answer is simple: eat (or don't eat) your freezer meals any way that you want. Use them for lunches, or dinners, or both. There isn't a wrong way! You could start out by eating them exclusively, and then space out your pre-made meals with your own home-cooked meals and meals from friends and family. If you eat them, and they keep you from having to cook, your prep is paying off!

How we used our meals

When we were in the NICU with our newborn son, our friends and family brought us food, so we didn't start eating our meals until we arrived home. Later, when my mother arrived, she took on more of the cooking. She sometimes watched the baby so I could cook, but we ate our frozen meals when we were too exhausted to do more than heat dinner up.

Sometimes we ate our meals for lunch, and sometimes for dinner. We also ate take-out occasionally for a treat, and we enjoyed a few outings to restaurants with our infant (who was still sleeping a lot at that point). After my mom left and I took over meal planning and prep again, our prepared meals played a backup role: I still made my meal plan every week, but every week included one or two nights of frozen meals. This made them last much longer, and it gave me a cushion in case I was too tired, or the baby didn't cooperate with my cooking schedule!

Sample Meal Plans

Below are two different suggestions for how to use your meals, and some accompanying meal plans. Keep in mind that the potential variations for the use of your meals are endless. Take your best guess at what will work well for your family and do that! The key idea in any meal plan is to vary your meals, especially your protein. Don't eat beef two nights in a row if you can help it. Boredom is the enemy!

The Exclusive Meal Plan

In this approach, you start eating your meals every single day for a month as soon as your baby is born – you decide not to cook at all so you can focus on your new family member. If friends and family bring over food, great, but if not, then you always have a hot meal ready to go.

A sample one-week Exclusive meal plan:

Sunday: **Frozen** Adobo Corn Chowder

Monday: **Frozen** Beef Ragu with Pasta and Frozen Kale
(blanched before cooking pasta)

Tuesday: **Frozen** Black Bean Soup

Wednesday: **Frozen** Sweet and Sour Chicken with Frozen Rice *(microwaved)*

Thursday: **Frozen** Split Pea with Ham

Friday: **Frozen** Traditional Beef Stew

Saturday: **Frozen** White Bean Cassoulet

The Adaptive Meal Plan

This approach is all about the natural flow of your postpartum life and how you work with it. Friends and family might bring food at first, and then that wanes, so you'll use frozen meals more as the weeks progress. Or your prepped food may play a critical role early on, but as the weeks go by, you want to do more cooking or (gasp!) eat out, so it acts as a back-up when the meal plan fails.

Mostly, I want to give you a sense of how these recipes can be used to support your family, no matter your lifestyle or activity level!

A sample two-week Adaptive meal plan:

Week 1

Sunday: **Frozen** Kasha with Beef Soup

Monday: **Frozen** Curry Vegetable Soup w/ Bread

Tuesday: **Frozen** Sweet and Sour Chicken w/ Frozen Rice

Wednesday: *Fresh!* Friends/Family bring dinner

Thursday: **Frozen** Black Bean Soup w/ Salad

Friday: *Fresh!* Get take-out

Saturday: **Frozen** Adobo Corn Chowder

Week 2

> **Sunday:** *Fresh!* Friends/Family bring dinner
>
> **Monday:** **Frozen** Chipotle Chili with fresh avocado and corn chips
>
> **Tuesday:** *Cook!* Roast chicken with potatoes
>
> **Wednesday:** *Cook!* Ramen with frozen veggies and leftover chicken
>
> **Thursday:** **Frozen** Asian Pork
>
> **Friday:** **Frozen** Traditional Beef Stew
>
> **Saturday:** **Frozen** White Bean Cassoulet

Meal Planning and Cooking with a New Baby

Despite having tons of amazing food in your freezer, you will at some point have to start cooking again. This will be easier if you were in the habit of cooking prior to your baby being born, but even if you weren't, it isn't too late to start new habits. After all, you'll want to keep feeding your family healthy and nutritious food even after your freezer meals are done, right? And before you know it, your baby will be old enough to start enjoying meals with you!

Entire books have been written on the subject of planning meals, cooking, and eating with a baby, so I'll leave you in the capable hands of other authors, but I wanted to give you a sense of how I plan my family meals so you have somewhere to start. It may sound time-consuming, but most of this takes just a few minutes of thought.

How I Plan Our Meals

Before we had a baby, I did my shopping on Sundays, so that's when I start my menu. Even if I go grocery shopping on a different day of the week, I still start my menu on Sunday, just for the sake of consistency.

I consider dinners first. Fridays are special, so we usually make pizza or gyoza (potstickers) or some other meal that feels fun and hasn't changed since before we had a kid. That handles one meal right off the bat.

We've always eaten leftovers for lunch, so I think about bigger meals to start the week, and I choose smaller meals with fewer leftovers for the middle and end of the week. This usually keeps us from entering the next week with a bunch of half-eaten dishes in the fridge, but I'll freeze the leftovers if it's obvious we aren't going to finish the food.

Second, I look at my calendar. I do most of the cooking, so I have to ask the question, "What's my week like?" Am I really busy with work or other obligations? Is Ben around at all in the evening? (If I ask, Ben will take over some of the cooking responsibilities.) How's my energy level? How creative am I feeling? Do I have some recipes I want to try, or should I just go with tried-and-true to keep it simple? What's on sale at the market? What am I craving? How has baby been sleeping? How much time do I have to cook? Your questions will likely differ slightly from mine, but it's essential to choose meals that are practical given the constraints of your life. Roast suckling pig probably shouldn't be on the menu.

Third, I look in my fridge and pantry. Is there anything I need to use up that I can plan a recipe around? Is it the end of the month, and therefore the end of the grocery budget? If either one is the case, I'll figure out meals that use what I have in the pantry and freezer, and minimize my expenditures by purchasing leaner cuts of meat and seasonal vegetables. I'll forgo fancy ingredients, or foods imported from far-off places, which tend to be more expensive.

Finally, I try to include variety throughout the week's meals, particularly in the protein source. I usually make a vegetarian dish, a fish dish, a chicken dish, and a beef dish. I don't eat lamb or veal, and we don't digest pork well, so I avoid those.

Above all, remember: A plan is often just a list of things that don't happen.

Don't be afraid to modify what you're doing. My meals often change nights, or they mutate! Squash and sausage soup turns into squash and sausage with kale hash because I don't feel like soup, and I'm the one making it. If you're cooking, you're in control!

Because my plans don't always work out, I have developed a list of 20-minute meals I can get together with barely any thought to use on days (or weeks!) when I have very little time or energy.

This list includes:

- **Fish tacos** (20 min in the oven, and I prep other ingredients while the fish cooks. We used to have this every Monday night because the fish was fresh after shopping.)

- **Pesto pasta with smoked salmon** (I usually have pesto in the freezer.)

- **Beef tacos**

- **Tofu green curry with rice** (much faster than it sounds)

- **Stir-fry** (contents will vary)

- **Red lentil soup**

- **Chicken soup**

- **Any pasta dish**

So: you're going to have a baby. How are you going to make sure you have healthy meals for your family now that running to the store is a pain the butt?

Well, it'll sure help if you're clear on...

– 7 –

how to cook it

In many families, mom cooks. That's the case for us, and if it's the case for you, you'll find some tips below for doing this prep work while pregnant. If someone else cooks in your family and you're the "someone else," the pregnancy tips might not be as topical.

How to Cook While Being Really Damn Pregnant

Take what you think you can do in a day and cut it in half. Seriously! You can't do what you used to. You move more slowly and your feet hurt. Sometimes you have Braxton-Hicks contractions every 10 minutes, or have to continually run to the bathroom. I pride myself on being able to cook for hours, but after seven months of pregnancy I could only reasonably pull off two recipes a day – and that was only if I started early enough!

Choose to cook in the time of day that you historically have the most energy. It will vary for everyone: I'm a morning person, but you might be a night person. Some women do CrossFit in their third trimester; I took a nap everyday. Don't start cooking when you're exhausted. Take sit-down breaks, or just make all your meals slow cooker meals so you don't have to get back  up to manage food on the stovetop! If you're especially tired, cut up veggies while sitting at the kitchen table. Make it as easy on yourself as possible. And remember to hydrate!

Above all, stay organized. Pregnancy brain is real, so write *everything* down. You aren't going to remember what ingredients you need at the grocery store or what time you started the soup. Set timers in the kitchen or on your phone, and post sticky notes in visible places to remind yourself what you should be doing. I once walked back and forth between the fridge and kitchen table three times to check for green curry paste because I couldn't remember what I was checking for by the time I made the trek.

There are six feet between my table and my fridge.

How to cook for tonight when you're cooking for next month

When I was cooking our freezer meals, we always taste-tested the recipe that night as our evening meal. I had a bit less to put in the freezer, but I didn't have to cook a whole separate dinner. Honestly, I don't know how else I would have done it – I was so tired that the only other viable option was going out. I highly recommend eating some of what you cook on the day that you cook it!

OK, enough with the warnings and caveats. Let's talk practical cooking techniques!

The Seven Basics of Slow Cooking

Slow cooking is fantastic because you can walk away from it! Once your prep is done and it's all in the pot, you can forget about it for the better part of the day and do other things (or just nap!) The only real downside is that slow cooked meals don't get browned by a hot pan, and so they don't develop the same depth of flavor as a stovetop meal. However, I've tuned these recipes to turn out great in the slow coo ker, so proceed with confidence!

1. Know your slow cooker!

Can you take out the cooker insert? It's a lot easier to wash that way. Can you set the time and temperature separately, or are they linked? Does it turn off automatically, or just "ding"? If you're looking to buy a slow cooker, try to get one that displays your cooking temperatures and times, and automatically sets itself to Warm when the time is up.

2. Don't skimp on the aromatics.

Aromatic seasonings – onions, garlic, spices, etc. – form the flavor base for most of these dishes, and if you don't use enough, the food will lack depth. You'll be fine if you're following these recipes, but if you're using your own recipes, be generous!

3. Cook it for the full time.

Most recipes taste better if cooked for a full 8 hours, especially beef. If you want extra flavor, you can also brown the beef with aromatics on the stovetop first, but keep in mind that it isn't necessary for tasty, tender slow-cooked beef.

4. Don't break up ground beef.

Let it cook in a block, then stir it later, or it will get mealy.

5. Cook chicken breast on Low for 6 hours maximum.

After the 6-hour mark, it gets dry and stringy. Chicken thighs don't have this problem because of the extra fat on them.

6. Thaw frozen foods before putting them in.

Partly frozen food can be OK, but chicken needs to come to 140° F after 2 hours in the cooker to be safe. You can start on High for a hour, and then turn it down to Low, but it's easier to just have mostly thawed food. *Never* put a whole frozen meal in the slow cooker.

7. Relax. You're not going to screw it up.

The Three Basics of Stovetop Cooking

Stovetop cooking is great if you're looking to get your prep done in less time with a deeper, richer result. The downside is that it takes more work, and you can't really walk away from it. But if that's OK, you'll usually end up with the best version of any recipe you try.

1. Prep everything before you start cooking.

Sometimes it makes you a bit less efficient, but it makes your job so much easier!

2. Brown your meat and aromatics.

Always brown your meat first, then remove it – we'll add it back later. Brown your onions next, then add your garlic and spices (only for 30 seconds, don't burn them!). Once your meat and aromatics are browned, we'll add in most of the other ingredients.

3. Wait to add your quick-cooking veggies and greens in the last few minutes.

Kale, chard, spinach, zucchini, etc. all soften very easily. Adding them at the end will keep them green and toothsome.

How to cook beans

Some of these recipes include beans, and there are many ways to prepare them. I personally prefer to soak and cook my own beans because it's cheaper and it gives me control over how much I make. You could also use canned beans, of course, and many cooks swear that soaking beans is a waste of time. Keep in mind, though: if you're using dried kidney beans, you *have* to soak them! Kidney beans contain a toxin called phytohemagglutinin that can cause stomach trouble, and you have to either soak or boil the beans for 10 minutes (then rinse them) to neutralize it. If you're not cooking with kidney beans, you don't really have to soak, but I recommend trying it once to gauge the results for yourself.

Soaking also reduces the gas-producing factors in legumes, and adding kombu (a Japanese seaweed) to your soaking beans will reduce the gas-producing factors even more. And rinsing your beans, even canned beans, will help break down the indigestible polysaccharides that coat the outside of the beans. Your gut bacteria eat those polysaccharides and produce gas!

If beans do give you gas, you can slowly train your body to tolerate them. Instead of making a big batch of chili and eating it three days in a row, defrost a smaller serving of chili, eat it for dinner, and then have a non-bean meal the next day. Repeat this process, chili day followed by non-chili day, for a week. Your gut will adapt to the increased legumes in your diet, you'll be able to eat more beans, and you won't blow up like a balloon in the process!

All issues of gas aside, though, beans are fantastic. They come packed with nutrition: protein, fiber, and lots of vitamins and minerals. They're low in fat, and they fill you up. What's not to like?

You often hear that you shouldn't cook beans with salt or acidic foods like tomatoes because the beans will remain hard. I've tried it both ways, and I've found that I prefer to salt my beans at the end to avoid any hardening. Try it, and see what feels right for you.

One thing that will always result in hard, uncooked beans is using old beans. If your beans are older than 6 months, for the sake of your sanity, throw them out and buy new beans. They're cheap, and you're on a timeframe – the hours you waste trying to get old beans to soften could be spent much better elsewhere!

Here are the basic steps to preparing dried beans of any type:

1. **Sort your beans.** Take out stones and discolored beans, then rinse.

2. **Soak your beans** (see below for how to quick-soak).

3. **Rinse your beans again.**

4. **Cook your beans!**

Quick-soaking dry beans

Don't want to let your beans soak overnight? Of course not! Fortunately, there's a simple way to get your beans ready to cook on the day you need them.

Measure out your beans and put them in a bowl (sort out any stones first). Pour boiling water over the beans, add a 4-inch strip of kombu, and let it sit for 1 hour. When done, pour the soaking water out and rinse the beans thoroughly. You can throw out the kombu after soaking.

Alternatively, soak the beans overnight in cold water with kombu, or for at least 8 hours during the day. Rinse thoroughly before using.

Approximately 2 ¼-cups of dried beans (1 pound) will become 6 cups of cooked beans, though quantities vary based on bean size.

Pressure-cooking your beans

For those of you with a pressure cooker, using it to batch-cook beans can be a huge time-saver. I pressure-cook several batches in a row and freeze them after they're cool. Always refer to your pressure cooker's instruction manual for specifics on how your pot works, but in general, these are the rules:

1. **Pressure-cooked beans must be pre-soaked.** Try the quick-soak method above!

2. **For every cup of dried beans add 3 cups of water,** as well as 1 tablespoon of vegetable oil to prevent foaming.

3. **Never fill your pressure cooker more than half full.**

4. **Don't pressure-cook lentils** or tiny beans like mung beans (unless you like eating mush).

5. **Cook for the full time** (see the chart below).

6. **Let the pressure come down naturally when cooking is done.**

Pressure-cooking Times by Legume	
Cook all these legumes on High	
Type of Legume	**Minutes**
Pinto beans	4 - 6
Black beans	8 - 10
Lentils	8 - 10
Great northern beans	8 - 12
Navy/Pea beans	10 - 12
Chickpeas (Garbanzos)	10 - 12
Kidney beans (Red)	10 - 12
All values courtesy of Fagor America, makers of fine pressure-cookers and other appliances.	
www.fagoramerica.com	

Slow cooking your beans

Slow cooking beans is nearly foolproof, and requires very little monitoring, yet results in perfect, creamy beans. You don't even need to soak your beans if you slow cook them (except for kidney beans, for the reason I mentioned above).

To cook beans in the slow cooker, place your beans in the pot and cover them with at least 2 inches of water. Make sure you leave at least half your slow cooker unfilled so the beans have room to expand, then cook them on Low for 6-8 hours. If you've never cooked beans in your slow cooker, start checking for doneness after 6 hours, as cook times will vary depending on the size of the beans and whether or not you pre-soaked them. Once your beans are cooked, drain them, rinse, and store. Simple!

Cooking your beans on the stovetop

When cooking beans on the stovetop, I recommend soaking them first because it will result in more even cooking. Goodness knows I've cooked them often enough without soaking, but unsoaked beans add to your cook time.

To cook beans on the stovetop, add your beans to a large pot and cover them with an inch of water (or two inches for unsoaked beans). Only fill your pot half full of beans and water so the beans have room to expand, then cook them for about 2 hours, depending on the size of the beans. You'll want to check for tenderness periodically; a well-done bean squashes easily between your tongue and the roof of your mouth. Take them off the heat before they start to crack, though! Once your beans are cooked, drain them, rinse, and store.

Freezing your beans

Once you've cooked up all your beans, nothing is easier than sticking them in the freezer for future use. Beans keep for about 6 months in the freezer, and any of the freezing methods we've discussed will work; my favorite is using half-full quart freezer bags to freeze 2 cups at a time. Whatever your method, make sure you measure your beans and label your containers!

Timesaver: How to Store Fresh Herbs

If you have more fresh herbs than you can possibly use at the moment, you can quickly and easily freeze them for later use. Simply fill the troughs of an ice cube tray ⅔-full with chopped herbs, then fill the remaining space with either oil or water.

Hardier herbs such as rosemary, sage, thyme, and oregano do well with the oil-freezing method, while softer herbs such as mint, basil, lemon verbena, and dill do better with water. Oil-frozen herbs can even be used "as-is" at the beginning of a dish when you sauté your aromatics – they come pre-oiled!

When the herbs are frozen, pop the cubes into a freezer bag and label it. Keep in mind that the more air there is around your herb-cubes, the more prone they will be to freezer burn, so use the smallest necessary bags and suck the air out of them to minimize exposure.

And however you choose to cook, you'd better know something about your...

– 8 –

ingredients

The recipes here use a variety of ingredients. None are exotic, but a few are less common, or misunderstood, and knowing your ingredients makes the whole process easier! For things like broth or stock, I've given you what I use in my kitchen, but there are many other options. For less-common ingredients like kasha, I've provided substitutions within the recipes themselves.

Stock and broth

The options are endless. You can make a rich, homemade bone broth, or you can buy it in a box; you can dissolve cubes in water or use a concentrate. The type of stock you use should be a kind that tastes good to you and meets your needs of price and convenience.

In my kitchen, I typically use **Better Than Bouillon**. It's a concentrate, which frees me to make as rich a broth as I would like. Don't get me wrong, a bone broth just can't be beat, but it takes time I don't always have. It's available at most groceries, and certainly online.

If food intolerances or allergies are an issue for you, Better Than Bouillon makes no claims of being gluten-free; however, their products list all the ingredients that contain gluten, and they use common terms like wheat, barley, oats, and rye. I find that their products do not trigger my own gluten intolerance.

Kasha

Even if you've never heard of kasha, chances are you'll love it. Kasha is roasted buckwheat, and it brings a robust, earthy flavor that balances the richness of beef and kidney beans. Buckwheat is chock-full of high quality fiber and protein, and it contains flavonoids that boost the antioxidant power of vitamin C. When you start to cook again, try kasha in a hash with mushrooms, potatoes, and kale.

Coconut milk

Made from the meat of mature coconuts, coconut milk has a consistency very much like cream, and it separates in the can, too. For our purposes, we'll be mixing the heavy cream on top with the lighter milk on bottom for a nice, smooth consistency. Coconut milk can often be found in the Asian section of your supermarket, and it can also be ordered online.

Curry powder

This is a sort of Westernized synthesis of some of the most common spices in Indian cooking. It varies somewhat by brand; most kinds contain some combination of coriander, turmeric, cumin, fenugreek, and red pepper, although other ingredients are common. I use it here not because it's "authentic," but because it's widely available and delicious! Experiment with different brands, or make your own for variations on a theme.

Tiny wine

O, tiny wine bottles, how do I love thee? Let me count the ways...

Well, if I'm honest, it really comes down to the fact that buying 4-packs of quarter-bottle-size wine is really economical for cooking. It also keeps me from having to either drink the rest of an open 750 mL bottle or let it go bad. I really hate letting wine go bad. Also, y'know, pregnant.

Good, cheap salt

My husband insisted this be part of the book: he loves salt, and our pantry has five or six kinds at any given time. And he has a point! There is no reason for you to use highly-processed salts (Morton, I'm looking at you) when there are inexpensive sea salts available at many groceries and online. And don't think good salt needs a

46

gourmet label; even cheap sea salt will impart a better flavor to your food than industrial table or kosher salts. Buy a couple cups and you'll have more than enough.

Beans and lentils

Beans and lentils (collectively, legumes) are fantastic, both from a culinary and nutritional perspective. In a dish, they provide color, texture, and a number of complex flavors; as I discussed earlier (see *Chapter 1: Basic Nutrition*), they're also a great source of dietary fiber, protein, vitamins, and minerals. They'll keep you full. And they're cheap!

However, If you keep your ears open, you'll hear an argument rage between home cooks who favor the convenience of canned beans and those who prefer to save money buying dried beans. Claims of flavor, texture, and wholesale pricing abound.

I don't have a dog in this fight; you can use either canned or dried, and it won't hurt my feelings. But because I want you to make an informed decision:

1. **Canned beans are packed in water, which makes up about half the weight of the can.** They may also be packed with salt – avoid those if possible, as they will add unnecessary salt to your recipes and your diet. Otherwise, rinse first. In one 15.5-ounce can, there are about 1⅓ cups of cooked beans, depending on the size of the beans.

2. **If your beans are already cooked**, you can just measure out 1⅓ cups of cooked beans for each can you would otherwise use.

3. **If you're measuring dried beans to substitute for canned**, use 1/5 of a pound of dried beans for every can in the recipe.

One last tip: if you're going to use dried beans, make sure to spread them out on a towel and check for stones and damaged beans before you soak them. You don't want chipped teeth!

Many of our recipes use smaller quantities of beans, which makes them easier to digest. However, if you worry about the gas-producing qualities of the humble legume, the previous chapter covers methods for reducing or eliminating that issue (see *Chapter 7: How To Cook It*)

Kombu

The Japanese answer to the gas-producing factors in beans! It's a seaweed, and when you soak or cook beans with it, it helps break down the undigestible polysaccharides that create gas in the intestine. Love it!

Canned tomatoes

I use a lot of canned tomatoes in my recipes. I tend toward good organic brands like Muir Glen, mostly for their superior flavor, but other brands work fine too. Costco even carries organic canned tomatoes that I use in cooked dishes, though I don't care for them in fresh dishes like salsa. All canned tomatoes are typically packed at the peak of freshness, which locks in essential ingredients, and because they're already cooked, they're higher in lycopene. Try using fire-roasted tomatoes to put some extra spice in your black bean soup!

Chipotle chiles and powder

Chipotle chiles (say *chip-oat-lay*) are smoke-dried jalapeños, and they provide a marvelous combination of savor and heat. There are dried chipotles, chipotles in adobo sauce, powdered chipotles, and chipotle chili powder (which contains chiles other than chipotles, too). Be forewarned: if you want to use chipotle chiles in adobo sauce, which have a lovely rich flavor, the only brand I've been able to find that isn't made with gluten is La Costeña.

Ume plum vinegar

This Japanese condiment is just what it sounds like: the distilled essence of sweet, sour, salty ume (say *oo-may*) plums in vinegar form. It's easily my favorite seasoning for soups, especially Coconut Chicken Soup, and it can be used to add depth and bite to all sorts of dishes.

Onions

Onions are indispensible for building the flavor base of soups and stews. However, not all onions are created equal, and knowing the difference can really help your cooking.

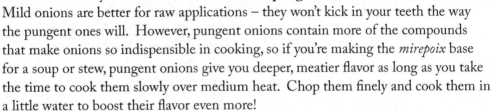

The thing to keep in mind about onions is that they come in two fairly different varieties: **mild** and **pungent**. Mild onions are better for raw applications – they won't kick in your teeth the way the pungent ones will. However, pungent onions contain more of the compounds that make onions so indispensable in cooking, so if you're making the *mirepoix* base for a soup or stew, pungent onions give you deeper, meatier flavor as long as you take the time to cook them slowly over medium heat. Chop them finely and cook them in a little water to boost their flavor even more!

Surprisingly, the color of an onion has little to do with the strength of its flavor, so you need to know what to look for. Mild onions can be recognized by their softer flesh (it gives a little, not a lot) and their wider, shorter necks. Pungent onions are rock-hard, heavy for their size, and typically have thick, dry, papery skins and long necks that have dried and shriveled.

Organic vs. Conventional

Oh, boy. This topic has become political, so I'll keep it short.

First, organic products can contain some "naturally derived" pesticides like Bt and rotenone, but typically contain much lower levels of pesticides than do conventionally grown crops. If you're worried about pesticides, the **Environmental Working Group** publishes a list of the 12 fruits and vegetables with the highest average levels of pesticide residue when grown conventionally (the **"Dirty Dozen"**), as well as a list of the 15 fruits and veggies with the lowest levels (the "Clean Fifteen"). Buy organic when in doubt, if pesticides concern you.

Second, organic products sometimes have a better balance of nutrients or fats. This varies widely, though, so you aren't guaranteed better nutrition from organic foods.

Third, organics are often much more expensive than their conventional counterparts, and this alone makes them an unreasonable choice for some families. Ultimately, eating organic is not as important as eating a balanced diet of vegetables, fruits, lean meats, and whole grains.

Fresh vs. Canned vs. Frozen

Fresh is best, so long as it's actually *fresh*: old, tired vegetables and fruits don't pack the nutritional punch of their frozen or canned counterparts, and even ripe produce loses its potency quickly. If you struggle to plan or use what you buy within days of buying it, fresh foods may not be for you.

However, canned foods are usually harvested at their peak ripeness, and canning preserves nutrients well. As long as you're selective, there's no reason to avoid them. The only real reason not to eat canned goods is potentially high salt content. Always check the sodium level and the ingredients list on the back of the can; if it has much added salt, expect to rinse the food before using it, or look for a different brand. Also, canned goods tend to have more soluble fiber. That can cause intestinal gas, so be forewarned. Overall, canned goods are an excellent choice.

Frozen goods have the distinction of being harvested at their peak freshness and being viable for long-term storage without added salt or preservatives like sodium benzoate. However, they have to be thawed properly to prevent bacterial overgrowth or spoilage, so take heed. Frozen foods are an excellent choice, so long as you use them safely.

How To Make Substitutions

Every recipe in this book is both gluten- and dairy-free, but that doesn't mean that I've made a whole bunch of exotic substitutions. Instead, I've chosen recipes that already required very little of either. However, some of you will want to adapt recipes of your own to freeze, and I'd like to make that as friendly a process as possible for the GF/DF folks who are prepping for a baby.

Dairy substitutions

  Use coconut oil for butter as a one-to-one substitute; be forewarned, it makes baked goods crispy. Otherwise, use ¾-cup of oil for each cup of butter in a baked good.

Coconut cream makes an excellent substitute for heavy whipping cream. For dairy-based spreads, I often use cashew cream; it's delicious, and I've included the recipe after the main recipes (see *Chapter 10: Side Dishes*).

Gluten-free grain substitutions

  Use kasha when a recipe calls for barley. The flavor is nuttier and more toothsome, which to my mind is an improvement.

Use rice when a recipe calls for pasta if you're going to freeze it. Pasta, almost uniformly, freezes very poorly, but gluten-free pasta freezes **terribly**.

The common gluten-free grains are rice, quinoa, amaranth, millet, corn, buckwheat (kasha), and sorghum. If you have celiac disease, you need to find supplies of these grains that are not made on shared equipment, as some gluten can be transferred from other grains during the milling process.

The gluten-containing grains are wheat (even emmer), spelt, barley, rye, and triticale.

Vegan/Vegetarian substitutions

 I've offered ways to make every single one of my recipes vegan, but generally speaking, if you want to make a recipe vegan, substitute vegetable broth for chicken or beef broth, and substitute beans, tofu, tempeh or meat substitute for the meat. All the the recipes are quite forgiving, so if you keep the proportions about the same (substitute 1 pound tofu for 1 pound meat), the recipes will be just as delicious as their meaty counterparts. Keep in mind that most imitation meats contain gluten!

Other ingredient substitutions

You'll notice the conspicuous absence of mushrooms, bell peppers, and lamb in all the recipes here. My family doesn't like those much, so I haven't included them. If you're a fan of any of those foods, though, feel free to introduce them! Keep in mind that mushrooms tend to increase the "umami" flavor of a dish – they make it meatier-tasting. Bell peppers add a layer of flavor, too, and lamb works well in place of beef.

So, what's the bottom line?

Make these recipes your own! If you don't like green beans, use broccoli. If you can eat dairy, feel free to use it. If you can eat gluten, you're welcome to use barley in place of kasha. If I've said it once, I've said it a thousand times: you aren't going to screw it up!

– 9 –

the recipes

Finally, we've reached the actual food!

How to use these recipes

My recipes are written in standard recipe format and contain all the pertinent details. I've cooked each recipe countless times, testing and testing again, but as most home cooks know, cooking is more art than science. I encourage you to use your judgement when it comes to meal preparation. You know what spices you like and don't like. You know what vegetables your family will eat. Use the foods you love, and ignore my suggestions if they don't make sense for your family.

I've measured the quantities each recipe makes, but your results may vary depending on the ingredients you use and the other vagaries of kitchen life. And I know I've said this before, but you aren't going to screw up your food. These recipes are very forgiving, so proceed with confidence!

Before Baby recipes appear longer than traditional recipes because I give you two different cooking options: *Stovetop* or *Slow Cooker*. Slow cooking is undoubtedly easier than stovetop cooking because you can just throw the ingredients in the bowl, but that won't necessarily get you the best possible version of each recipe. Every recipe will turn out well with either cooking method, but I've indicated if one method is superior.

For some slow cooker recipes I suggest microwaving your aromatics (onions, celery, etc.), but this isn't required. And while many crockpot aficionados swear by browning your meat before adding it to your cooker, I've never found the added flavor to be worth the cleanup. Stovetop cooking, on the other hand, demands sautéing and browning because the food isn't cooking as long. I've been served stovetop soup where the ingredients were just thrown in the pot willy-nilly, and the results were a tasteless disaster. Do the work if you're cooking atop the stove – it's worth it.

"Salt to taste"

Despite the current backlash against including the instruction "salt to taste" in a recipe *(Didn't know there was a controversy? Well there is, and battle lines have been drawn!)* I've included it for two reasons:

One, many of the recipes call for broth or stock of some kind, and I don't know what type you're using. Some store-bought broths are saltier than others, so it's best if you adjust the seasoning of your recipe after it's cooked.

Two, you swell up like a balloon after you give birth – no joke – and you don't want a bunch of extra salt while you still have "cankles." It may also take a while for your taste preferences to stabilize, and while it's easy to add salt to a dish, it's impossible to get it out!

Whenever I cook, I almost always leave the food slightly undersalted before I freeze it, then encourage my family and guests to salt the food to their liking. It just seems simpler that way!

How to modify quantities

I've done my best to standardize the quantity of food each recipe will produce. I want you to have a good estimate of how much food you have socked away before baby is born! However, if you want to modify the quantities, simply halve or double the ingredients.

A note about serving sizes: I can't predict how much you'll eat after your baby is born, but I will tell you that breastfeeding makes you ravenous. Once-ladylike appetites begin to resemble those of large, jungle-dwelling carnivores! I've estimated a serving to be 2 cups of soup or stew, or 1 cup of any dish served over rice or pasta. Don't be surprised if you want even more!

How I developed the recipes

All these recipes were developed, prepared, and tested in the kitchen of our 800-square-foot Seattle apartment. I am not a chef, and I do not have access to a professional kitchen. My slow cooker is super old (both handles are broken off – I asked for a new one for Christmas, but didn't get it), and while I have a nice set of pots and pans, no esoteric cooking devices were used in the production of these meals.

We prepared all the food in this book for our own use. We cooked it all before we had our baby. We took pictures of it. Then we ate it.

That's not to say the recipes haven't been extensively tested. I developed these recipes over years of home cooking, nutrition counseling, blogging, and consulting, and they were tested again prior to publication by a dedicated host of home cooks, most of them parents themselves. They're tried-and-true.

However, the photos are not perfect; the food is not professionally styled. The potatoes are chopped cockeyed, and they got a little mealy from sitting in the soup. The colors aren't as pristine as they could be because it took days sometimes to get to shooting a picture. However, these pics are an excellent representation of what real food made in a real kitchen by real people looks like.

And it tastes **good.**

adobo corn chowder

Makes 4 quarts

Prep Time 20 minutes

Cook Times

    Stovetop 1 hour

    Slow Cooker 6 hours on low

Whether you make it with kielbasa or go vegetarian instead, this spicy and flavorful soup will be a hit with everyone in the family. For a less spicy soup, use fewer chiles. I like this soup with whole kernels of corn, but Ben prefers it blended – either way, it's delicious! And if you're gluten-intolerant, be sure that your chipotle chiles in adobo sauce don't contain wheat.

Ingredients

1   tablespoon olive oil

1   medium onion, diced

2   stalks celery, diced

2   medium carrots, diced

2+ chipotle chiles in adobo sauce, chopped OR ½+ teaspoon chipotle chile powder

10 ounces kielbasa, diced

1   pound (~3 medium) red potatoes, peeled and diced

8   cups frozen corn, thawed

8   cups chicken broth

Optional Garnish

Cilantro

Cashew Cream

Sour Cream

To Make the Chowder on the Stovetop

Sauté the Aromatics Heat the olive oil over medium heat in a large pot. When the oil is shimmering, add the onion, carrots and celery. Cook until soft, stirring occasionally, 5-10 minutes. Stir in the chipotle chiles in adobo sauce and the kielbasa, and cook for an additional 3-5 minutes.

Make the Soup Add the potatoes, corn and chicken broth. Cover and bring to a boil, then reduce heat to low. Simmer covered for approximately 30 minutes, until all the flavors are combined.

> *Optional* Use an immersion blender to puree some of the soup in the pot.

To Make the Chowder in the Slow Cooker

In a medium bowl, mix together the onion, carrots, celery and olive oil, and microwave on high 5 minutes, stirring halfway through. Alternatively, sauté for 5-10 minutes on the stovetop until soft. Place the onion/carrot/celery mixture in the bowl of your slow cooker, along with the chipotle chiles in adobo sauce, kielbasa, potatoes, corn and broth. Cook on low for 6 hours.

> *Optional* Use an immersion blender to puree some of the soup right in the crock pot.

To Make it Vegetarian Replace the chicken broth with vegetable broth and omit the kielbasa.

To Make it Veggie-licious Add 10 ounces of thawed frozen kale or green beans during the last 30 minutes of cooking time.

asian pork

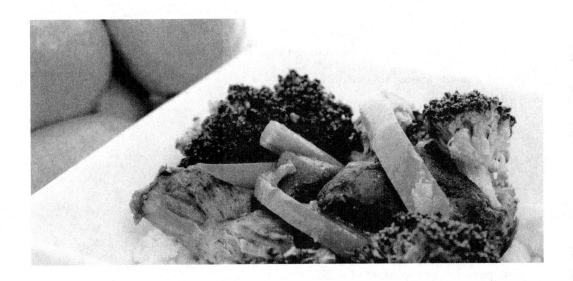

Makes 2 ½ quarts *(to be served with rice)*

Prep Time 20 minutes

Cook Times

    Slow Cooker 6 hours on high   *(No stovetop version)*

We love all kinds of Asian food in this house, and I adore this recipe for its simplicity and flexibility. Substitute boneless skinless chicken thighs for the pork if pig isn't your preferred beast, and serve this dish over reheated frozen brown rice or noodles – the addition of the carbohydrate will take the quantity of the finished dish from 2 ½ quarts to 4 quarts.

Ingredients

½ cup gluten-free hoisin sauce

4 tablespoons low-sodium tamari

½ teaspoon ground ginger

4 cloves garlic, minced or put through a garlic press

2 teaspoons toasted sesame oil

¼ teaspoon cloves

2 pounds boneless pork shoulder or pork butt, trimmed and cut in half

½ onion, diced

2 carrots, diced

4 ounces green beans, cut into one inch pieces

1 red bell pepper, cut into strips

~¾ pound broccoli, cut into 1-inch pieces

To Make it in the Slow Cooker

In a medium bowl, combine the hoisin sauce, tamari, ground ginger, garlic, toasted sesame oil and cloves. Stir and set aside. In the bowl of your slow cooker, place the pork, onion and carrots, and then gently pour in the sauce, mixing to distribute. Cook on high for 5 hours and then add the green beans, bell pepper, and broccoli. Cook on high for an additional hour.

To Make it Vegetarian Substitute 2 pounds of extra-firm diced tofu for the pork butt.

To Make it Veggie-licious Add 2 diced zucchini and 10 ounces of kale.

beef ragu

Makes 3 quarts *(to be served over pasta)*

Prep Times

> *Stovetop* 20-30 minutes with pre-cooking

> *Slow Cooker* 15 minutes

Cook Times

> *Stovetop* 2 hours

> *Slow Cooker* 8 hours on low (preferred) **or** 4 hours on high

Pasta is a favorite dish in our house, and even before we had a baby I kept some ragu in the freezer for quick weeknight meals. This recipe is rich in tomato-y goodness but light on veggies because I like to blanch kale or green beans in the boiling water before I cook the pasta. If you want more veggies in the original recipe, simply add them in the last half-hour of cook time.

Ingredients

1 pound ground beef

2 teaspoon olive oil *(Stovetop only)*

½ onion, diced

2 large (or 4 medium) carrots, diced

~2 cloves garlic, minced or put through a garlic press

1 teaspoon dried basil

1 teaspoon dried oregano

½ cup red wine

2 28-ounce cans diced tomatoes

1 15-ounce can tomato sauce

1 bay leaf

1 teaspoon sea salt

1 teaspoon sugar (or equivalent sweetener)

To Make the Ragu on the Stovetop

Brown the Beef   Heat a 6-8 quart pot on the stove over medium heat. Add the ground beef and cook, stirring occasionally, until brown. Remove the beef to a bowl.

Sauté the Aromatics   Add the olive oil to the pot and heat for 1 minute, then add the onion and carrot. Turn down the heat to slightly below medium and cook, stirring occasionally, until the vegetables are soft. Add the garlic, oregano and basil and cook 30 seconds, stirring occasionally, until the garlic is fragrant but not burned. Deglaze the pan with red wine, turning the heat up to medium high. Stir and scrape the brown bits off the bottom and cook until the wine is reduced by half.

Cook the Soup   Add the beef, tomatoes, tomato sauce, bay leaf, sea salt and sugar. Cover and bring to a boil, then reduce heat to low and simmer for 2 hours, or until the sauce seems done, stirring occasionally. Serve over pasta and blanched vegetables (either fresh or frozen will do).

To Make the Ragu in the Slow Cooker

Place the ground beef, onion, carrots, garlic, basil, oregano, red wine, diced tomatoes, tomato sauce, bay leaf, salt and sugar in the bowl of a 6-quart slow cooker. Give it a quick stir, being careful to not completely break up the ground beef. Cook for 8 hours on low (preferred) or 4 hours on high. Serve over pasta and blanched fresh or frozen vegetables.

To Make it Vegetarian Eliminate the ground beef; otherwise, follow the instructions.

To Make it Veggie-licious Add diced zucchini and/or green beans in the last 30 minutes of cooking.

black bean soup

Makes 4 quarts

Prep Times 1 hour bean soak
(optional), 15 minutes assembly

Cook Times

> *Stovetop* 30 minutes for cooked
> beans, 1 hour for uncooked beans
>
> *Slow Cooker* 8 hours on low OR
> 4 hours on high

*This warming and slightly spicy soup
is a breeze to make either on the stove
or in a slow cooker, and it freezes
superbly. The trick to a deep, rich
flavor is chipotle powder or chipotle
chiles in adobo sauce. I have trouble
finding gluten-free chiles in adobo
sauce, so I use the chipotle powder,
but if you can find them or don't need
to be gluten-free, use the whole chiles!
Garnish with cilantro, a plain, non-
dairy yogurt, or cashew cream (see
Side Dishes).*

Ingredients

12	cups cooked black beans, rinsed and sorted
½	stick of kombu
2	tablespoons olive oil *(Stovetop only)*
1	medium onion, diced
4	medium carrots, diced
3	stalks celery, diced
1	red bell pepper, diced
4	cloves garlic, crushed
~1	teaspoons chipotle powder OR 2 allergy-friendly chipotle chiles in adobo sauce, chopped
1	teaspoon cumin
1	teaspoon oregano
1	bay leaf
1	15-ounce can fire-roasted tomatoes *(substitute **diced** if sensitive to spice)*
8	cups chicken broth
	Juice of one lime
	Salt to taste

To Soak the Beans

Measure out black beans and place in a bowl. Pour boiling water over the beans, add kombu, and let sit for 1 hour. When done, pour soaking water out, throw away kombu and rinse beans thoroughly again. Alternatively, soak overnight or at least 8 hours during the day in cold water with kombu. Remove kombu, rinse and proceed with recipe.

To Make the Soup on the Stovetop

Sauté the Aromatics In a 6- or 8-quart stockpot, heat olive oil on medium heat. Add onion, carrots, celery and red bell pepper and sauté for 10 minutes, stirring occasionally. Stir in the garlic, chipotle powder or chipotle chiles, cumin, and oregano, cooking for 30 seconds, until the garlic is fragrant but not burned.

Assemble the Soup Add the bay leaf, fire-roasted tomatoes, beans, and broth, and combine thoroughly. Cover pot and bring soup to a boil. Once at a boil, reduce the heat to medium low and simmer for 1 hour. Stir in the lime juice and add salt as needed.

To Make the Soup in the Slow Cooker

In the bowl of your slow cooker, place the soaked and rinsed beans, onion, carrots, celery, bell pepper, garlic, chipotle powder or chipotle peppers, cumin, oregano, bay leaf, fire roasted tomatoes and broth. Cook 8 hours on low or 4 hours on high. Add the lime juice and salt to taste.

> *Optional* Replace the dried beans with rinsed, canned, beans or precooked beans. Use 5 15-ounce cans or 6-7 cups precooked beans. Reduce broth to 4 cups and reduce cooking time to 30 minutes.

To Make it Vegetarian Use vegetable broth in place of chicken broth.

> *NOTE* We've tried this recipe with water in place of broth, and while it can be done, it doesn't possess the same depth of flavor.

To Make it Veggie-licious Double the recommended vegetables or add your own. I suggest kale and zucchini added in the last 10 minutes of cooking on the stovetop or the last 30 minutes in the slow cooker.

chicken peanut stew

Makes 2 ½ quarts *(to be served over rice)*

Prep Time 20 minutes

Cook Times

    Stovetop 30 minutes attended, plus 1 hour unattended

    Slow Cooker 6 hours on low

This rich and creamy stew is flavorful without being aggressive, and the lime you add at the end really rounds it out. Don't be daunted by the list of ingredients, especially if you're using a slow cooker—it's mostly spices, and the result is worth it! Garnish with cilantro and whole peanuts for a bit of crunch, and serve over brown rice for a filling meal.

Ingredients

1   tablespoon olive oil *(Stovetop only)*

1   medium onion, diced

1   green Thai chile, finely chopped

1   medium red or orange bell pepper, diced

1   teaspoon dried ginger

1   teaspoon coriander

1   teaspoon turmeric

½   teaspoon cumin

⅛   teaspoon cloves

1   14-ounce can diced tomatoes, including juice

2   tablespoons tomato paste

¾   cup creamy peanut butter

½   cup water

2   teaspoon salt

2   pounds boneless skinless chicken thighs

~2 pound sweet potatoes, peeled and cut into 1-inch dice

10 ounces fresh green beans, chopped into 1-inch pieces

Juice of one lime

Optional Garnish

Cilantro

Peanuts

To Make the Stew on the Stovetop

Sauté the Aromatics   Heat the olive oil in a large pot over medium heat until shimmering. Add the onion and cook 10 minutes, stirring frequently, until soft. Add the Thai chile, bell pepper, ginger, coriander, turmeric, cumin and cloves, and sauté 30 seconds, stirring continuously.

Deglaze the Pan   Add the tomatoes, stirring to remove the browned bits from the bottom, and then add the tomato paste, peanut butter, water and salt. Turn the heat down to low and cook for 2-3 minutes, until the peanut butter melts and the sauce combines.

Make the Stew   Add the sweet potatoes and chicken, and stir. Bring to a slow boil, cover, and reduce to simmer. Cook for 45 minutes, or until the chicken is cooked through. Stir in the green beans and cook an additional 15 minutes. Remove the pot from the heat and break up the chicken using a spoon, then add the lime juice. Add salt and pepper to taste. Serve over brown rice.

To Make the Stew in the Slow Cooker

Place the onion, Thai chile, bell pepper, ginger, coriander, turmeric, cumin, cloves, diced tomatoes, tomato paste, peanut butter, water, salt, sweet potatoes and chicken in the slow cooker. Cook on low for 5 hours, and then add the green beans and cook for an additional hour. Turn off the slow cooker and break up the chicken with a spoon. Add the lime juice, and salt and pepper to taste. Serve over brown rice.

To Make it Vegetarian   Use tofu or tempeh in place of the chicken.

To Make it Veggie-licious   Add thawed frozen spinach with the green beans!

chipotle chili

Makes 4 quarts

Prep Time 20 minutes

Cook Times

    Stovetop 20 minutes attended + 2 hours unattended

    Slow Cooker 4 hours on high **or** 8 hours on low

This is one of those recipes that works best when cooked slowly, so I suggest saving your stove time for red lentil soup or coconut chicken soup, which are slightly tastier on the stovetop. This chili gets spicy quickly, so opt for less chile powder if you are spice-sensitive. If you don't have chipotle chile powder, use regular chile powder in its place.

Ingredients

1 tablespoon vegetable oil *(Stovetop only)*

1 pound ground beef

1 onion, diced

3 ribs celery, diced (1 cup)

~2 carrots, diced (1 – 1 ½ cups)

1 4-ounce can green chiles, drained

~3 teaspoons chile powder

~3 teaspoons chipotle chile powder

1 teaspoon cumin

1 teaspoon oregano

3 cloves garlic

1 teaspoon salt

1 28-ounce can diced tomatoes

2 15-ounce cans kidney beans, drained and rinsed OR 3 cups cooked kidney beans

1 15-ounce can tomato sauce

1 red bell pepper, diced

8 ounces green beans, cut into 1-inch pieces (2 cups)

1 cup frozen corn

Optional Garnish

Cilantro

Diced avocado

Shredded cheddar cheese

Sour cream or cashew cream

To Make the Chili on the Stovetop *(NOT preferred)*

Brown the Meat   Heat the oil in a large pot over medium heat until shimmering and then add the ground beef. Cook until brown, stirring occasionally, about 10 minutes. Remove to a plate.

Sauté the Aromatics   In the fat that remains in the pan, cook the onion, celery and carrot until brown, stirring occasionally, about 10 minutes. Add the diced green chiles, chile powder, chipotle chile powder, cumin, oregano, garlic and salt. Sauté until the spices are fragrant, about 30 seconds.

Cook the Chili   Add the diced tomatoes, kidney beans and tomato sauce. Cover and bring to a boil, then reduce the heat to low and simmer for about 1 hour 45 minutes.

Add the Vegetables and Adjust the Seasonings   Taste the chili and add more salt if needed. Toss in the red bell pepper, green beans and corn and cook an additional 15 minutes.

To Make the Chili in the Slow Cooker *(preferred)*

In the bowl of your slow cooker, place the ground beef, onion, carrots, celery, green chiles, chile powder, chipotle chile powder, cumin, garlic, salt, diced tomatoes, kidney beans, tomato sauce, red bell pepper, green beans and corn. Give the dish a gentle stir to combine all ingredients. Cook on low for 8 hours or high for 4 hours.

> *Optional*   For crunchier veggies, put the red bell pepper, green beans and corn in the slow cooker during the last hour of cooking.

To Make it Vegetarian   Add 2 cans of black beans in place of the ground beef.

To Make it Veggie-licious   Double the veggies, or try adding some peas and zucchini.

coconut chicken soup

Makes 4 quarts

Prep Time 20 minutes

Cook Times

Stovetop 50-60 minutes

Slow Cooker 6 hours on low

This is, hands down, Ben's favorite soup. We make it with 2 teaspoons of green curry paste because I'm a spice wuss, and then Ben adds more curry to his bowl. I prefer to add toasted sesame oil instead. Either way, we've found that you need a little more green curry when making this soup in the crock pot.

For extra creamy goodness, replace the second can of coconut milk with coconut cream if you can find it. It's how my family prefers the soup!

Ingredients

1 tablespoon olive oil *(Stovetop only)*

½ onion, diced

2 large carrots, diced

4 cloves garlic, minced

¼ teaspoon red chile flakes

3+ teaspoons green curry paste *(4+ teaspoons in the slow cooker)*

8 cups chicken broth

2 chicken breasts (approximately 1 pound)

½ cup brown rice

10 ounces or 1 bunch kale, torn into bite-size pieces

8 ounces or 1 head broccoli , chopped into bite-size florets

8 ounces green beans, cut into 1-inch chunks

2 14.5-ounce cans full fat coconut milk *(use coconut cream if you can find it)*

1 lime's juice

Optional Garnish

Ume plum vinegar   Toasted sesame oil

Cilantro   More green curry paste

To Make the Soup on the Stovetop

Sauté the Aromatics Heat the olive oil in a large soup pot over medium heat. Add the onion and carrots, turning down the heat to slightly below medium, and sauté for 10 minutes, stirring occasionally, until the onions and carrots are soft. Add the garlic, red chile flakes and green curry paste and cook for 30 seconds, until the spices are fragrant but not burned.

Make the Soup Add the chicken broth and bring soup to a boil. Add the chicken breasts and brown rice, cover, bring back to a boil, and then turn down to simmer. Cook the chicken breasts 15-20 minutes, until cooked through, and then remove to a plate with tongs. Cook the rice an additional 10 minutes and then add the kale, broccoli and green beans. Simmer uncovered for 10 minutes more, until the veggies are tender but not mushy. While the veggies cook, shred the chicken into bite-size pieces, and then add it back into the soup along with the coconut milk and lime juice.

To Make the Soup in the Slow Cooker

Place the onion, carrots, garlic, red chile flakes, green curry paste, chicken broth, chicken breasts, and brown rice in the slow cooker. Cook on low for 5 hours. Add the kale, broccoli, green beans and coconut milk (or coconut cream) and cook for another hour. Turn off the slow cooker and remove the chicken breasts to a plate. When they are cool enough to handle, shred them into bite-sized chunks and return to the soup. Stir in the lime juice.

> **NOTE** This soup will not suffer one bit if you add the vegetables at the beginning of the cook time, they'll just be softer. Definitely still add the coconut milk (or coconut cream) and lime juice at the end.

To Make it Vegetarian This soup is just as tasty when veggie! Substitute vegetable broth for the chicken broth and use 16 ounces firm tofu in place of the chicken. Add the tofu when you add the green vegetables. You could even bump up the brown rice to ⅔ cup for a bit more substance.

To Make it Veggie-licious Add zucchini and/or cauliflower with the other vegetables.

country chicken stew

Makes 4 quarts

Prep Time 20 minutes

Cook Times

> *Stovetop* 30 minutes attended, plus 1:40 unattended

> *Slow Cooker* 6 hours on low

When we first came home from the hospital, this was my favorite stew. It's mild and nourishing, and after a week in the "food desert" of the NICU, all the vegetables were just what my body needed to recover from giving birth. This is a sweeter stew that can be eaten alone, but pairs well with a salad dressed in a tangy vinaigrette.

Ingredients

2 tablespoons vegetable oil *(Stovetop only)*

3 pounds boneless skinless chicken thighs, trimmed

1 onion, minced

6 cloves garlic, minced or put through a garlic press

1 tablespoon tomato paste

½ teaspoon dried thyme

½ cup dry white wine

4 carrots, peeled and diced

4 cups chicken broth

2 bay leaves

~2 pounds sweet potatoes or yams, peeled and cut into 1-inch pieces

1 cup frozen peas

1 large zucchini, diced

½ pound green beans, cut into 1" pieces

10 ounces kale, chopped

To Make the Stew on the Stovetop

Brown the Chicken   Heat the vegetable oil in a large pot over medium heat until it shimmers. Place half the chicken, smooth side down, in the pan, and cook for 5 minutes. Flip chicken with a pair of tongs and cook for an additional 3 minutes. The chicken will be browned but not completely cooked through. Remove the chicken to a plate, and repeat with the rest of the chicken.

Sauté the Aromatics   Turn the heat to slightly below medium and add the onions to the oil/chicken fat remaining in the pan. Sauté for about 10 minutes, stirring occasionally, until the onions are brown and soft. Add the garlic, tomato paste and thyme, and sauté, stirring constantly, for an additional 30 seconds until the garlic is fragrant but not burned. Turn the heat back up to medium high and deglaze the pan with white wine, scraping up the browned bits (they're delicious!).

Cook the Stew   Add the carrots, chicken, and chicken broth. Cover the pan and bring to a boil. Turn down the heat to low, keeping the stew at a simmer, and cook for about 1 hour 40 minutes.

Add the Vegetables   Break up the chicken with a spoon – it should come apart easily. Add the sweet potatoes and cook for 10 minutes, then add the zucchini, kale and green beans, and cook for additional 10 minutes. Adjust seasoning as needed.

To Make the Stew in the Slow Cooker

Place the chicken thighs, onion, garlic, tomato paste, thyme, white wine, carrots, chicken broth, and bay leaves in the slow cooker. Cook for 5 hours on low. Add in the sweet potatoes, peas, zucchini, green beans and kale, and cook for an additional hour, or until the vegetables are cooked through. Remove the chicken to a platter and allow to cool slightly, then shred and return to the pot. Add salt and pepper as needed.

To Make it Vegetarian   Substitute vegetable broth for chicken broth, and use 3 cans of white beans for the chicken (cannellini are lovely). Skip the browning step.

To Make it Veggie-licious   You can add more veggies if you like, but it's chock-full already!

curry vegetable soup

Makes 4 quarts

Prep Time 15 minutes

Cook Times

Stovetop 50 minutes

Slow Cooker 8 hours on low **or** 4 hours on high

This is one of the most flexible soups I make. Everything about it is easy to tweak, from the amount of spice you use to whether it contains meat. Try adding 4 bone-in, skinless chicken thighs and cook for 8 hours in the slow cooker – the chicken will be falling off the bone! You could even add 4 cups of broth instead of 6 for more of a stew and less of a soup. And absolutely don't omit the lime juice – it's crucial for a well-rounded, finished soup!

Ingredients

1 tablespoon olive or vegetable oil *(Stovetop only)*

½ large onion, diced

2 large carrots, peeled and diced

4 cloves garlic, minced or put through a garlic press

3 tablespoons curry powder *(use less if sensitive to spice)*

1 teaspoon dried ginger

½ teaspoon red chili flakes *(use less if sensitive to spice)*

10 ounces frozen cauliflower, thawed

10 ounces frozen cut green beans, thawed

10 ounces frozen green peas, thawed

1 15-ounce can garbanzo beans, drained and washed

2 medium (~1 pound) potatoes, scrubbed and diced

1 tablespoon tamarind paste OR sugar

6 cups chicken broth

1 14-ounce can coconut milk

Juice of 1 lime

Salt to taste

Optional Garnish

Cilantro

To Make the Soup on the Stovetop *(NOT preferred)*

Sauté the Aromatics   Heat the olive oil in a large soup pot over medium heat until it shimmers. Add the onion and carrots, stirring gently. Turn the heat down to just below medium and sauté for 10 minutes, stirring occasionally. Add the garlic, curry powder, dried ginger and red chili flakes, and cook another 30 seconds, until the spices are fragrant but not burned.

Make the Soup   Add the cauliflower, green beans, green peas, garbanzo beans, potatoes, tamarind paste OR sugar, and chicken broth. Bring to a boil, cover and turn down to a simmer. Cook 30 to 45 minutes, until the potatoes are soft and the flavors have begun to meld. Remove from heat and add the lime juice.

To Make the Soup in the Slow Cooker *(preferred)*

Place the onion, carrots, garlic, curry powder, dried ginger, red chili flakes, cauliflower, green beans, green peas, garbanzo beans, potatoes, tamarind paste OR sugar, and chicken broth in the bowl of your slow cooker. Cover and cook 8 hours on low or 4 hours on high. Remove from heat and add the lime juice.

To Make it Vegetarian   Use vegetable broth instead of chicken broth.

To Make it Veggie-licious   Add even **more** of the recommended veggies or go outside the box: try bell peppers or zucchini!

kasha with beef soup

Makes 4 quarts

Prep Time 20 minutes

Cook Times

    Stovetop 2 hours (attended)

    Slow Cooker 4-6 hours on high OR 8-10 hours on low

This is my new favorite soup because it reminds me of beef with barley, a soup I loved as a child and can no longer eat because of the gluten. If gluten isn't a problem for your family, feel free to use barley instead!

To get around cutting up the chuck roast, buy pre-cut stew meat or use ground beef. If you opt for ground beef, simply place the chunk of beef in the slow cooker whole. Don't break it up until halfway through cooking or it will get mealy. And while I say the wine is optional, it really adds an extra bit of meaty "umami" flavor to the soup. Don't skip it if you don't have to.

Ingredients

2   tablespoons vegetable oil *(Stovetop only)*

1   pound chuck roast or stew meat, cut into 1-inch chunks

½   onion, diced

2   cloves garlic, minced or put through a garlic press

½   cup red wine (optional but recommended)

1   28-ounce can of diced tomatoes, plus juice

1   15-ounce can of kidney beans, drained and rinsed

1   10-ounce bag of frozen corn, thawed

1   10-ounce bag of frozen cut green beans, thawed

½   cup kasha

1   teaspoon dried basil

1   teaspoon dried oregano

1   bay leaf

1   quart beef broth

Salt to taste

To Make the Soup on the Stovetop

Brown the Beef   Heat your stockpot and vegetable oil over medium heat and then add the beef, browning on all sides. Browning will take about 10 minutes. Remove the beef to a plate.

Sauté the Aromatics   In the remaining oil (add more if needed), brown the onions, stirring occasionally, about 10 minutes. Add the garlic and stir continuously until the mixture is aromatic, about 30 seconds. Deglaze the pan with the red wine, reducing it by half.

Make the Soup   Add the beef, tomatoes, kidney beans, corn, green beans, onion, kasha, basil, oregano, bay leaf, and beef broth. Give the soup a quick stir, cover with a lid and bring to a boil. Turn your soup down to medium-low and let cook, stirring occasionally for 2 hours, or until the beef is falling apart.

Make the Soup in a Slow Cooker

In the bowl of your slow cooker, gently place the chuck roast, onion, garlic, red wine, tomatoes, kidney beans, corn, green beans, kasha, basil, oregano, bay leaf and beef broth. Give it a quick stir to combine, and then cook 4-6 hours on high **or** 8-10 hours on low.

To Make it Vegetarian Lose the beef, use 4 cans (or ~5 cups) of cooked kidney beans, and use vegetable broth in place of beef broth.

To Make it Veggie-licious Add 2 chopped carrots when you're cooking the aromatics!

red lentil soup

Makes 5 quarts

Prep Time 15 minutes

Cook Times

    Stovetop 30 minutes

    Slow Cooker 4 hours on high **or** 8 hours on low

Red lentils are a tasty, quick-cooking legume that you can easily make into soups or curries. As with all legumes, you want to season them with salt at the end of the cooking time, otherwise they may stay firm and not cook all the way through. This recipe requires an 8-quart pot for stovetop cooking – if you don't have one, divide the ingredients between two pots. This is such a quick soup that I prefer to make it on the stovetop and reserve the slow cooker for a meat-based dish.

Ingredients

1 tablespoon olive oil *(Stovetop only)*

1 onion, diced

2 large (or 4 medium) carrots, peeled and diced

4 medium cloves garlic, minced or put through a garlic press

3 teaspoons garam masala

2 teaspoons curry powder

½ teaspoon dried ginger

~⅛ teaspoon cayenne

1 red bell pepper, chopped

1 medium head cauliflower, cut into bite-sized pieces

3 cups red lentils, sorted and rinsed

6 cups chicken broth

1 head (8 ounces) kale, stems removed and torn into bite-sized pieces

2 14-ounce cans organic coconut milk

Salt and pepper to taste

Optional Garnish

Cilantro

To Make the Soup on the Stovetop *(preferred)*

Sauté the Aromatics Heat the olive oil in a large pot over medium heat until shimmering. Add the onion and carrot and cook 10 minutes, stirring frequently, until soft. Add the garlic, garam masala, curry powder, dried ginger and cayenne, and sauté 30 seconds, stirring continuously.

Make the Soup Add the lentils, bell pepper, cauliflower and broth. Bring to a boil, cover and reduce to simmer. Cook for 15-20 minutes, or until the lentils are cooked through but not mushy. Stir in the kale and coconut milk and cook an additional 5 minutes. Salt and pepper to taste.

To Make the Soup in the Slow Cooker *(NOT preferred)*

Microwave the Aromatics   Place the olive oil, onion and carrot in a heat-proof bowl and microwave on high for 4 minutes. Remove from the microwave and stir, then add the garlic, garam masala, curry powder, dried ginger and cayenne. Microwave on high for an additional minute.

Alternatively, just throw everything in the slow cooker! The flavor won't be quite as smooth, but the results will still be scrumptious.

Make the Soup   Place the lentils, aromatics and broth in the bowl of your slow cooker. Cook on low for 8 hours or high for 4 hours. During the last 30 minutes of cooking, add the red bell pepper, cauliflower, kale and coconut milk. Salt and pepper to taste.

To Make it Vegetarian   Use vegetable broth instead of chicken broth.

To Make it Veggie-licious   Double the amount of kale!

sweet and sour chicken

Makes   *Stovetop* 4 quarts   *Slow Cooker* 3 quarts

Prep Time 20 minutes

Cook Times

    Stovetop ~25 minutes, attended

    Slow Cooker 6 hours on low

This recipe is lovely either in the slow cooker or on the stovetop. Why does the stove-top recipe make more? The vegetables stay a bit crisper and therefore lose less water.

The chicken will take on more of the sweet and sour flavor in the slow cooker, but by allowing the stovetop chicken to sit in the sauce while it cools, the dish will meld and become just as flavorful. I prefer chicken thighs for this dish because the extra fat keeps the chicken tender (and thighs are cheaper), but feel free to substitute chicken breasts if you prefer.

For the stovetop version, I recommend preparing all your ingredients and having them at hand before yous start cooking. This is called "mise en place," and it's very helpful when stir-frying. The process will go very quickly!

Ingredients

To Make the Dish

2+ tablespoons vegetable oil

3 pounds boneless skinless chicken thighs

½ large sweet onion (8-12 ounces), cut into strips

12 ounces broccoli (2 large heads), cut into bite-size pieces

8 ounces green beans, cut into 1-inch pieces

2 large carrots, cut on the bias

1 large red bell pepper, sliced into strips

1 8-ounce can bamboo shoots, drained

1 14-ounce can pineapple chunks plus juice

To Make the Sauce

½ cup chicken broth

½ cup brown sugar

½ cup seasoned rice vinegar OR white vinegar

¼ cup low-sodium tamari

3 tablespoons tomato paste

4 medium cloves garlic, put through garlic press or minced

1 teaspoon dried ginger (or 2 teaspoons fresh ground ginger)

½ teaspoon red chili flakes

2 tablespoons lemon juice

To Make it on the Stovetop

Prepare the Mise en Place Trim the fat from the chicken thighs and then slice into half-inch wide strips against the grain. Cut up the onion, broccoli, green beans, carrots and bell pepper. Open the bamboo shoots and drain them. Open the pineapple can and set aside.

Make the Sauce In a medium bowl, whisk together the chicken broth, sugar, seasoned rice vinegar, tamari, tomato paste, garlic, ginger, red chili flakes and lemon juice. Set everything beside the stove, because cooking will go quickly!

Brown the Meat In a large pot, heat the oil over medium-high heat until hot. Brown the chicken in two batches, about 4 minutes each, and then remove to a plate. It's OK if the chicken is a little pink when you take it out of the pan – it will cook while resting and cook more when added back into the pan.

Sauté the Vegetables Add the onion, broccoli, green beans and carrots to the oil that remains. Add ¼ cup water (or more if necessary) so the vegetables don't stick to the pan. Cook for about 5 minutes. They should still be very crisp.

Finish the Sweet and Sour Chicken Add the red bell pepper, bamboo shoots, pineapple and sauce. Cook an additional 5 minutes, stirring occasionally. If you are using a 6-quart pot, your pot will be very full. Don't worry, the vegetables will cook down, but stir very gently!

Serve with brown rice.

To Make it in the Slow Cooker

Toss the whole chicken thighs in the slow cooker, along with the onions, carrots, chicken broth, sugar, seasoned rice vinegar, tamari, tomato paste, garlic, ginger, red chili flakes and lemon juice. Cook for 5 hours on low. Add the broccoli, green beans, bell pepper, bamboo shoots and pineapple. Cook for another hour on low. Gently mash the chicken thighs with the back of a spoon to break them up.

Serve with brown rice.

To Make it Vegetarian Use 32 ounces of extra firm tofu in place of the chicken.

To Make it Veggie-licious Add two zucchinis and a 4-ounce can of water chestnuts with the bell pepper, bamboo shoots and pineapple toward the end of cooking.

split pea with ham

Makes 4 quarts

Prep Times 15 minutes

Cook Times

    Stovetop 1 hour 10 minutes

    Slow Cooker 8 hours on low **or** 4 hours on high

Growing up, I loved Progresso's split pea with ham soup, and while I wouldn't touch the stuff now (have you looked at the ingredient list?), this soup reminds me of my childhood. The split peas will thicken and become creamy once they are refrigerated, and they'll stay that way when you reheat them, so there's no need to puree this soup. This recipe is slightly lighter on the vegetables, so I like to serve it with a mixed green salad (gotta love those pre-washed mixes) and an oil-and-vinegar dressing.

    NOTE There's no delicate way to say this, so I'll just spit it out. While we love this soup, split peas make us gassy, so I freeze this one in smaller batches. We only eat one or two bowls apiece before moving on to something different. One bowl is fine, but four bowls in a row puts the hurt on us. I recommend you do the same unless your family is blissfully unaffected by legumes.

Ingredients

1	tablespoon vegetable or olive oil *(Stovetop only)*
1	medium onion, diced
4	cloves garlic minced or put through a garlic press
2	large (or 4 medium) carrots, peeled and diced
4	large stalks celery, diced
1½	pounds split peas (3 cups), washed and sorted
5	ounces (1 cup) diced uncured ham OR 1 pound ham shanks
8	cups chicken broth
1	teaspoon dried oregano
1	bay leaf
	Salt to taste

To Make the Soup on the Stovetop *(NOT preferred)*

Sauté the Aromatics   Heat the olive oil in a large soup pot over medium heat until it shimmers. Add the onion, carrots, and celery, stirring gently. Turn the heat down to just below medium and sauté for 10 minutes, stirring occasionally. Add the garlic and cook another 30 seconds, until the garlic is fragrant but not burned.

Make the Soup   Add the split peas, hams, broth, oregano and bay leaf. Bring to a boil, cover and then simmer for 45 minutes to 1 hour, until the peas are tender. Add salt if needed.

To Make the Soup in the Slow Cooker *(preferred)*

Place the onion, garlic, carrots, celery, split peas, ham, oregano and salt in the slow cooker. Slowly pour in the chicken broth and gently stir. Cook for 8 hours on high or 4 hours on low.

To Make it Vegetarian   Eliminate the ham and use vegetable broth in place of the chicken broth.

To Make it Veggie-licious   Add a diced medium red potato, green peas, or any other vegetable your heart desires.

traditional beef stew

Makes 4 quarts

Prep Time 20 minutes

Cook Times

    Stovetop 30 minutes attended, plus 2 hours unattended

    Slow Cooker 8 hours on low **or** 4 hours on high

When I was growing up, my mother would make the most amazing beef stew, and I've tried to re-create it for you here. Normally I'd pack it with veggies, and I've given you some great options at the end of the recipe, but after my baby was born I just wanted good ol' home cookin', so instead of putting the veggies in the stew, I ate it with bag salad and called it a night!

In my opinion, this recipe works well in both the slow cooker and on the stovetop, but as with all slow cooker beef recipes, I highly recommend you cook it for at least 8 hours on low to get the most tender, delicious beef possible.

Ingredients

1 tablespoon vegetable oil *(Stovetop only)*

~3 pounds chuck roast or stew beef, cut into 1-inch pieces

1 medium onion, diced

4 medium cloves garlic, minced or put through a garlic press

1 pinch of cardamom powder

½ cup red wine

3 large (or 5 medium) carrots, cut into 1-inch pieces

1 28-ounce can diced tomatoes, juice included

4 cups beef broth

2 teaspoons Worcestershire sauce

2 bay leaves

1½ pounds red potatoes, cut into 1-inch pieces

Salt and pepper to taste

To Make the Stew on the Stovetop

Brown the Beef Heat the vegetable oil in a large pot over medium heat. Add half the beef and brown on all sides, about 10 minutes. Remove to a plate and repeat with the other half of the beef.

Sauté the Aromatics Add the onion to the pot (with a touch more oil if necessary) and sauté until soft, about 10 minutes. Add the garlic and cardamom and cook an additional 30 seconds, until the garlic is fragrant but not burned. Deglaze the pan with red wine and cook for about 2 minutes, scraping the browned bits off the bottom of the pan.

Make the Stew Add the beef back into the pot, along with the carrots, tomatoes, broth, Worcestershire sauce and bay leaves. Cover, bring to a boil, and then turn down to low. Simmer for about 1 hour 40 minutes, then add the potatoes and cook an additional 20 minutes. You can add the potatoes at the beginning of the cooking time, but they'll retain their shape better during freezing if they are cooked at the end. Adjust seasoning as needed.

To Make the Stew in the Slow Cooker

In the bowl of your slow cooker, place the beef, onion, garlic, cardamom, red wine, carrots, tomatoes, broth, Worcestershire, bay leaves and potatoes. Cook 8 hours on low OR 4 hours on high.

To Make it Vegetarian   Replace the beef with 3-4 cups of beans of your choice; kidney beans are especially delicious, but make sure to soak them! *(see Chapter 7: How To Cook It)* Use vegetable broth in place of the beef broth.

To Make it Veggie-licious   At the end of the cooking time, add peas, green beans, and/or mushrooms.

white bean cassoulet

Makes 4 quarts

Prep Time 20 minutes

Cook Times

Stovetop 1 hour 20 minutes

Slow Cooker 8 hours on low **or** 4 hours on high

The French word "cassoulet" can refer to this particular kind of chunky stew, or to the curve-bottomed pot it is often cooked in. This is a wintertime favorite in our household, although cooking it in the slow cooker during the summer doesn't heat up the house and provides a hearty and nourishing meal after a long day at the lake! Any additional veggies pair well with this dish, but we really love green beans. I typically use chicken sausage for this dish, but if you prefer the authentic Italian sausage, go right ahead!

Ingredients

2   pounds chicken Italian sausage, casing removed

1   tablespoon olive oil *(Stovetop only)*

1   medium onion, diced

~4   cloves garlic, minced or put through a garlic press

1½   cups bold red wine *(like Cabernet Sauvignon or Merlot)*

~4   medium carrots, roughly chopped

2   14-ounce cans white beans, drained and rinsed

1   pound red potatoes, chopped into large dice

28   ounces diced tomatoes, in juice

1½   teaspoon thyme

1   bay leaf

1½   teaspoon oregano

1   teaspoon salt

To Make it on the Stovetop

Brown the Sausage   Heat a cassoulet or oven-proof stock pot over medium heat. Add sausage and brown, then remove it from pan to a plate.

Saute the Aromatics   Turn the heat to slightly below medium and add the olive oil. Allow it to heat for 1 minute, then add the onions and sauté for about 10 minutes, stirring occasionally, until the onions are brown and soft. Add garlic and cook until fragrant but not brown, about 15 seconds.

Deglaze the Pan   Add the red wine to the pot, scraping bottom of pot with a wooden spoon to free browned bits.

Cook the Cassoulet   Toss the sausage back into the pot, and add carrots, beans, potato, tomatoes, thyme, bay leaf, oregano and salt. Bring to a boil, then reduce heat to medium-low and simmer for about an hour, or until all ingredients are soft but not mushy.

To Make it in the Slow Cooker

Place the sausage, onion, garlic, red wine, carrots, beans, potatoes, tomatoes, thyme, bay leaf, oregano and salt in the slow cooker. Cook on low for 8 hours OR high for 4 hours.

To Make it Vegetarian   Eliminate the sausage and use 1 pound of mushrooms in its place. Increase the quantity of white beans to 3 cans.

To Make it Veggie-licious   Add 10 ounces of green beans at the start of the cook time.

– 10 –

side dishes

Most meals aren't one thing alone – most include a garnish, a side, or some little element that rounds out the main dish. Sometimes it's just a sliced piece of fruit or a cooked grain. Other times, it's a dipping sauce or a salsa. The main dishes in *Before Baby* have a few sides of their own, and I want to show you how to make them here.

Some of these sides, like brown rice, you may have been making so long that they're second nature, and if you have your own way of cooking it, don't let me dissuade you! But if you've never made hummus at home, or enjoyed the spice called *garam masala* in a dip, then I encourage you to try these little recipes. Each one is quick and guaranteed to please.

And they all freeze beautifully!

hummus

Makes 4 cups

Prep Time 15 minutes

Hummus is a quick and easy protein-filled snack you can eat on the go or in the comfort of your home. Pair it with fresh chopped veggies, including carrots, bell peppers, and cucumbers.

Ingredients

2   15-ounce can chickpeas (garbanzo beans), drained and rinsed

2   large cloves garlic

½   cup tahini

4   tablespoons fresh lemon juice

1   teaspoon salt

~¼   cup olive oil

~¼   cup ice water

    Smoked paprika for garnish

To Make It

Add chickpeas to the bowl of your food processor and pulse until roughly chopped. Then add garlic, tahini, lemon juice, and salt, and pulse until all ingredients are chopped and combined. Through the top, drizzle in the olive oil while blending. Continue blending, drizzling in ice water until the consistency is loose. When desired consistency is reached, continue blending for ~3 minutes to smooth the texture.

Garnish with paprika and serve with chopped veggies. Freeze in ½-cup servings in either glass jars or plastic containers.

masala lentil dip

Makes 4 cups

Prep Time 20 minutes

Ingredients

- 3 cups cooked lentils (fresh or canned), drained and rinsed
- 3 tablespoons tomato paste
- 2 tablespoons lemon juice
- 2 tablespoons tahini
- 2 cloves garlic
- 1½ tablespoons brown sugar
- 1½ teaspoons curry powder
- 1 teaspoon garam masala
- 1 teaspoon salt
- ½ teaspoon paprika
- ½ teaspoon turmeric
- ¼ teaspoon ground ginger OR ½ teaspoon fresh ground ginger
- ¼ teaspoon cayenne
- ¼ cup olive oil

This dip is my version of a bean spread they used to sell at Trader Joe's. It's sweet and spicy and completely addicting! Any type of lentil will do, but I've been using canned black lentils. Don't be intimidated by the list of ingredients – it's mostly just spices.

To Make It

In the bowl of your food processor or blender, place the lentils, tomato paste, lemon juice, tahini, garlic, brown sugar, curry powder, garam masala, salt, paprika, turmeric, ground ginger and cayenne. Puree until chopped and starting to blend, then drizzle in the olive oil as the food processor blends. Puree another 2 minutes until the dip is smooth.

Freeze in ½-cup servings in either glass jars or small plastic containers. Serve with chips or fresh chopped vegetables.

brown rice

Makes 3 cups

Prep Time 20 minutes

Many people are dissuaded from eating brown rice because of the cooking time, but you can solve that problem by pre-cooking and freezing your own! Much cheaper than the supermarket frozen rice, homemade precooked rice allows you to choose your variety, and gives you control over your quantities.

You cook brown rice with twice as much water as you have rice: use a 2-to-1 ratio of water to rice. Because the math is so simple, you can make a much larger batch than I've shown below, if you so desire.

We eat many different varieties of rice at our house. I often make long grain brown rice as a staple, but I love eating jasmine rice with Thai food, and basmati rice with Indian food. If you've never tried the many different varieties of rice out there, you owe it to yourself to start exploring!

Ingredients

1 cup brown rice

2 cups water

   Pinch of salt *(optional)*

To Make It

Bring rice, water and salt to a boil, then cover and cook on medium low for about 40 minutes, or until all the water is absorbed. To check if the rice is done, don't stir the rice! Instead, lift the pot and tilt it slightly to the side. If you see water, you need to continue cooking your rice. Let the rice sit covered off the heat for 10 minutes, then fluff with a fork. Freeze 2 cups at a time in 1-quart freezer bags.

quinoa

Makes 3 cups

Prep Time 25 minutes

Quinoa (keen-wah) is an ancient Andean grain that's become popular in recent years for its high protein content. Nutty and chewy, quinoa can be used in place of rice in any recipe, and it's delicious added to salads. It comes in brown or red varieties; the differences in flavor are negligible. And one more thing: if you aren't purchasing pre-washed quinoa, it's crucial that you rinse it before cooking to wash off the bitter chemicals (called saponins) that coat the outside. Once it's rinsed, it's ready to cook!

Ingredients

1   cup quinoa, rinsed

2   cups water

Pinch of salt (optional)

To Make It

Bring the quinoa, water and salt to a boil, then cover and reduce heat to medium low. Cook for about 20 minutes, or until the quinoa is done. To check if the quinoa is done, don't stir the quinoa! Instead, lift the pot and tilt it slightly to the side. If you see water, then you need to continue cooking. When finished cooking, let the quinoa sit covered off the heat for 10 minutes, then fluff with a fork. Freeze 2 cups at a time in 1-quart freezer bags.

cashew cream

Makes 3 cups

Prep Time 8 hour soak,
plus 10 minutes of active prep

*Cashew cream makes a lovely
substitute for dairy cream. It works
wonderfully drizzled in soups or
mixed with salsa in a dip. To make
cashew sour cream, mix lemon juice
with your cashew cream to taste.*

Ingredients

2   cups raw cashews

8   cups boiling water, plus ½ cup cold
    water

½   teaspoon salt

To Make It

In a medium glass or plastic bowl
(don't use metal), soak the cashews
in boiling water for 8 hours. Drain
and place the cashews in the bowl of
your food processor or blender.
Add cold water and salt, and pulse
to puree, scraping down the sides.
Once ingredients are mixed,
puree for 5 minutes until the cashew
cream is completely smooth, adding
cold water 1 tablespoon at a time as
needed. The cream will thicken up
when refrigerated. Freeze in ½-cup
servings in glass jars or plastic
containers. Cashew cream will keep
for up to a week in the refrigerator.

– 11 -

breakfast and snacks

Breakfast with Baby

Preparing breakfast with a newborn can be extremely challenging, but eating that first meal of the day will help keep your energy level high. Breastfeeding mothers also have increased caloric needs from producing breast milk, and everyone can use wholesome food to compensate for some of the sleep deprivation. Skipping meals, especially breakfast, isn't a good option for new parents!

I recommend either eating breakfast before your little one wakes up or, more likely, eating it when he goes down for his first nap. I kept a bowl for nuts and dried fruit next to my nursing spot for the first several weeks; it would keep my blood sugar up if my son demanded to nurse right when I wanted breakfast. This trick was especially helpful if I got hungry in the middle of the night.

You don't want to be any more irritable than you have to be at a 3:00 a.m. feeding!

Nutritionally, you want to aim for a breakfast that includes both whole grains and protein for sustained energy. Fruit and veggies are a bonus, but can be difficult to include during those first few weeks.

My breakfast suggestions:
- **Instant or pre-cooked oatmeal with nuts**
- **Whole-grain toast with peanut butter**
- **Hard-boiled eggs**
- **Banana and almond butter**
- **Protein smoothie**

Snacking with Baby

There are a lot of ways to grab a snack even though your little one wants your attention. Some of them require forethought and some don't, but none take much time or energy. Expect to eat them all with one hand!

My snack suggestions:

- **Nuts and dried fruit**
- **Hard-boiled eggs**
- **Apples and peanut butter**
- **Yogurt**
- **Granola bars** (choose wisely, see below)
- **Rolled-up lunchmeat**
- **Pre-cut veggies and hummus**
- **Premade sandwiches**
- **Edamame** (soybeans in the pod)

When do you prep these?

Choose a time when your little one is napping, or when you have help, then prep a bunch of snacks at once so you have a variety to choose from. My favorite is the edamame! You'll have to restock once every few days, but the convenience of having snacks at hand is well worth it.

How long will these snacks keep?

Every snack is different, so you'll have to use all your senses to see when food is good to eat. Apples and sandwiches usually won't keep for more than a day, but most of the other snacks will be good for 3-5 days. If it looks funky, don't eat it – the last thing you want with a newborn is food poisoning!

What snacks should you avoid?

Chips, cookies, candies – basically avoid anything that's sweet, salty, or fatty, but empty of nutrients. You're going to be tired, and when you're tired you crave calories, especially sugar and fat. Junk food fits the bill perfectly as far as that craving is concerned! But we call these foods "junk" for a reason: they provide a short-term energy boost, but they cause you to crash (in the case of sugar) and overeat (in the case of fat). You'll need about 500 extra calories a day if you're a breastfeeding mother, but you want high-quality, nutrient-dense foods, not junk. You'll feel better in the short term, and lose the baby weight faster, too!

It's also a good idea for mom to avoid foods with lots of preservatives. While there aren't many studies investigating dyes and preservatives in breast milk, we have to assume some are getting through, and there are several studies indicating the dangers of some food colorings in young children. Stick to whole foods as best you can and you will be doing your family a great service.

the last word

So, what's left to say?

How about... ***Get to it!***

Peel off a sticky note and write down the recipes that sound best for your family. Take a look at your freezer and pull the old food out. Take out your calendar and count the days left before your baby comes!

You can absolutely do this. There's no question in my mind, because I've done it, and so have many of my readers! It's just a series of steps, and if you start with the first one that seems sensible to you, you'll be on your way before you know it.

The cooking and freezing process is an incremental one. If you're anything like me, the process taken as a whole feels pretty daunting, so it's very important that you remember: ***one piece at a time.*** You will open the freezer before you look at it. You will look at it before you take anything out. And you will take something out before you decide to keep it or throw it away.

Give yourself permission to do one thing at a time, especially if pregnancy is sapping your physical or mental energy. I'm not just speaking to moms-to-be here, either. The knowledge that you have a baby on the way can be very energizing, but my husband found himself worrying a lot in the last trimester of my pregnancy, and it wore on him. If you need to take a break, take a break.

If you run into difficulty, remember: **Reassess. Adapt. Begin again.**

After all, that's the parent's way!

acknowledgements

Writing a book, like having a baby, is a team sport.

Thank you, first, to our families. You know who you are, and you know we might not have made it this year without you. We cannot properly express our ongoing gratitude in any language.

Next, to all our friends in the big bad city, thank you for casseroles and food bars in the NICU, and for cat- and dog-sitting. You were a crack in the iron walls that seemed to surround the hospital.

Thank you also for eating what we put in front of you. You made marvelous guinea pigs.

A big thank you to Deb, Angie, and Lauren for being our first line of defense against obfuscation, inaccuracy, and dumb mistakes in draft after draft. You were kinder than we deserved.

And, as is usually the case with anything in the age of the internet, *Before Baby* was helped on its way by the many other authors, editors, and self-publishers on the web whose freely-given advice proved invaluable. To those who have gone before us: *we salute you.*

about autumn

Autumn Hoverter, MS, RDN is a board-certified dietitian, a mother, and a cook. She lives in Seattle, Washington with her husband Ben, her son Teo, her dastardly dachshund Duncan, and two surly sister cats. In her spare moments, she's hard at work on her next book.

Follow Autumn on Facebook at www.facebook.com/foodwise and on Twitter at @foodwiserd.

To learn more about what she has to offer, visit autumnhoverter.com.

And don't forget to visit www.beforebabybook.com for updates to the book and answers to lots of your questions!

CPSIA information can be obtained
at www.ICGtesting.com
Printed in the USA
FSOW03n1105211217
42663FS

9 781517 343422